The Weiser Field Guide to
ghosts

The Weiser Field Guide to
ghosts

Apparitions, Spirits, Spectral Lights, and Other Hauntings of History and Legend

Raymond Buckland

WEISER BOOKS
San Francisco, CA / Newburyport, MA

First published in 2009 by
Red Wheel/Weiser, LLC
With offices at:
500 Third Street, Suite 230
San Francisco, CA 94107
www.redwheelweiser.com

ISBN: 978-1-57863-451-4
Library of Congress Cataloging-in-Publication Data available upon request.
Typeset in Adobe Jenson and Priori Sans
Cover photographs © istockphoto.com
Cover illustrations © Anne Brush
Original illustrations on pages 8, 23, 30, 36, 40, 47, 60, 68, 75, 80, 94, 98, 107,
110, 114, 119, 124, 139, 140 and 161 © 2009 by Anne Brush
Illustrations on pages 65, 66, 104, 129, 135, 164 and 165 © Miss Mary
Illustration on pages 87 © Pepin Press
Photographs on pages 11, 59, 79, 91, 109, 142, 177, 189 © Dreamstime
Photographs on pages 38, 69, 76, 82, 113, 130, 138 © istockphoto.com
Photographs on pages 19, 27, 49, 89, 88, 101, 121, 127, 133, 153, 166 © Veer

Printed in Canada
TCP
10 9 8 7 6 5 4 3 2 1
The paper used in this publication meets the minimum requirements of the
American National Standard for Information Sciences—Permanence of Paper for
Printed Library Materials Z39.48-1992 (R1997).

For Tara

The way to find out whether or not anything exists is to depend on the testimony of the ears and eyes of the multitude. If some have heard it or some have seen it, then we have to say it exists. If no one has heard it and no one has seen it, then we have to say it does not exist. So, then, why not go to some village or some district and inquire? If from antiquity to the present, and since the beginning of Man, there are men who have seen the bodies of ghosts and spirits and heard their voices, how can we say that they do not exist?

—Mo Tzu, Chinese philosopher 470–391 BCE

Contents

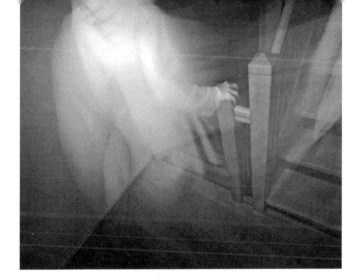

Introduction

Everybody loves a ghost story. Why? Probably because we all like to be frightened . . . though only when we know we're actually safe! Ghosts themselves don't *have* to be frightening (returned loved ones or pets are not, for example), but it's the *idea* of a ghost that thrills and chills. Some of the most famous ghost stories are in Charles Dickens's *A Christmas Carol*, Shakespeare's *Hamlet*, and Oscar Wilde's *The Canterville Ghost*. Popular movies, such as *Ghost* and *The Ghost and Mrs. Muir*, have added their impact. And today's television reality ghost-hunting shows have burgeoned into ghost-hunting clubs and societies scattered over the Internet.

So what *is* a ghost? It's a visual or auditory occurrence that is out of the ordinary, unexplainable by traditional criteria. The word comes from the Old English *gǎst*. There have been various definitions: "the apparition of a dead person," "an energy field that makes itself known by assuming the shape of a person," "the spirit of a person who was once alive," "an incorporeal being."

Ghosts are known around the world, by all peoples of all ages. They have been showing up since the beginning of recorded history. There's tremendous variety to ghosts, as will be seen. Among the different types are ancestral ghosts, battlefield ghosts, noisy ghosts, and even animal ghosts. There are orbs and flashes of light, ghostly mists, brilliant squiggly lines of energy that appear on photographs. There are ghost trains, cars, airplanes, and horse-drawn carriages.

It is said that the belief in ghosts grew out of the universal human need for assurance of survival after bodily death. If death is the end of everything; if time stops dead in its tracks for the deceased, then there would be no such thing as a ghost. But the appearance of a ghost signals that death is *not* the end; that some form of energy connected to the deceased continues.

In general, there are two types of ghosts: those that are seen and those that are heard. However, the form that the visual ghost takes varies tremendously, from the appearance of a much-loved but deceased dog to a floating light that cannot quite be pinpointed. There are ghosts of known deceased people and animals, and there are ghostly appearances by unknown spirits, some of them otherworldly. Europe, Australia, Japan,

Polynesia, India, in addition to America . . . all countries have their ghosts and spirits.

It used to be that the dead were buried in winding sheets (a shroud, or cloth in which the body was wrapped); this led to the depiction, by artists, of a ghost dressed in a white sheet . . . think of the cartoon character Casper the Friendly Ghost! Yet most "real" ghosts are seen dressed much as they appeared when alive.

Many ghosts are seen at places where they experienced a traumatic occurrence, or where they died, or—alternatively—where they had known great happiness. Such events are cause for the deceased to be loath to leave, to move on "into the light," and is generally an indication that the spirit is either unaware that death has occurred or is simply reluctant to accept the fact. There are individuals and groups, here on earth, who work specifically to help such earthbound spirits.

Not all ghosts are of the transparent variety! Many appear as dense as when they were alive. And whether solid or transparent, a lot of ghosts have been photographed. Most such photographs come about accidentally, with inexplicable images appearing in what should have been quite ordinary photographs. In 1861, a Boston photographer named William Mumler was at the studio of a photographer friend (Mrs. H. F. Stuart's Photographic Gallery) and was amusing himself with the equipment. He wanted to take a photograph of himself, so he placed a chair and focused the camera on it. His method—typical of the time—was to focus, then remove the cap covering the lens and run forward to take position standing beside the chair, holding still long enough for the camera equipment to trip and take the picture. When Mumler developed the plate, he found that there was a young girl sitting on the chair beside him . . . and that he could see the chair through her. He subsequently wrote on the back of the photograph, "This photograph was taken of myself, by myself, on Sunday, when there was not a living soul in the room beside me—so to speak. The form on my right I recognize as my cousin, who passed away about twelve years since."[1] This was the start of spirit photography. Mumler's wife Hannah, incidentally, was a Spiritualist clairvoyant and healer.

As well as other "ghost portraits," a tremendous number of fraudulent photographs were taken, with the perpetrator indulging in double exposures and other photographic tricks. Today, however, with the advent of infrared and, more especially, digital cameras, trickery is technically much more complicated. It can still be used to produce results—in fact the results can be even more amazing than of old—but it takes knowledge and skill. The "classic" photographs of ghosts, from the past, have been examined by experts and proven not to have been tampered with.

[1] William H. Mumler, *The Personal Experiences of William H. Mumler in Spirit-Photography*. Boston: Colby and Rich, 1875.

Another name for a ghost is an *apparition* This, in fact, is the term generally preferred by parapsychologists. Contrary to popular opinion, apparitions are not always of the dead; they can be appearances of the astral bodies of the living.

When there are wars, with many people killed, there are large numbers of ghost sightings recorded. Young men and women killed in battle frequently appear to their loved ones at the very moment of death. Shortly after the Society for Psychical Research was founded in 1882, an attempt was made to collect firsthand reports of apparitions. The majority of these turned out to be of the "crisis" variety. The full report was published in book form, in 1886, as *Phantasms of the Living*.

Whole battles have been seen in ghostly form, with the apparition of fighting men visible—sometimes to a large number of people—many miles from the scene of the battle. When a group of people have a collective sighting, invariably the observers see the apparition from different viewpoints, depending upon where they are standing at the time. It is, therefore, as though they are seeing the actual event rather than a projection of it, as in a movie scene. One person may see a particular figure full face while another, standing somewhere else, may see a profile.

Some ghosts appear as though on a regular schedule. This seems to apply especially to religious figures, such as the Lady of Lourdes and the similar appearances of the Lady of Medjugorje and the various Marian apparitions. As many as one in thirty apparitions are of the religious type (often referred to as "visions"). Such visions are very slow to be accepted by the Roman Catholic Church. There also seem to be "fashions" to such visions. A. R. G. Owens (*Man, Myth and Magic*) says, "In the Middle Ages visionaries saw saints and martyrs and, in certain limited circles, apparitions of the child Jesus were extremely frequent. Later, visions of the suffering and wounded Jesus or of his Sacred Heart were favored. In recent times the Virgin Mary has almost monopolized the field."

Some ghosts have been showing up regularly for many years. The famous "Brown Lady of Raynham Hall" is one. She died in the mid-1700s and has been seen (and photographed) descending the hall's wide staircase regularly ever since. Another regular is the ghost of Anne Boleyn, the second wife of England's Henry VIII and mother to the first Queen Elizabeth, who is frequently seen near Wakefield Tower; part of the Tower of London. Boleyn also haunts Hever Castle, her home in Kent, and Bollen Hall in Cheshire. Another of Henry's wives, Catharine Howard, haunts Hampton Court Palace.

The site of an appearance by a ghost is known as a *haunting*. Although hauntings are usually associated with old buildings, there are many that are in modern houses, apartments, and hotels. They are also in the open, where there are no structures. Ghosts seen at Native American burial grounds are a case in point.

Scratching, rapping, knocking, voices, and similar are the trademarks of auditory ghosts. The birth of modern Spiritualism came about through such a one. On Friday, March 31, 1848, in Hydesville, New York, the two young sisters Catherine (Kate) and Margaretta Fox, together with their parents, were frightened by the constant rappings that came on the walls and ceiling of their small cottage. Eventually Kate challenged the spirit to "do as I do" and clapped her hands three times. The spirit immediately responded with three raps. This was the start of a lengthy sequence of questions and answers—the first intelligent, two-way conversation between the living and the dead. The ghost turned out to be that of a murdered peddler named Charles B. Rosna, whose remains were later found buried in the basement of the house.

In this book I have tried to place the many types of ghosts into categories (for example, historic ghosts, animal ghosts, poltergeists, and so on), but there are the inevitable crossovers. For example, ghosts listed under one specific category may also appear as harbingers of death, or as prophetic, or otherwise. Some listed as "spirits" may also be animal ghosts, and so on. For easier reading, I have tried not to make too many cross-references, but there will be the occasional duplication.

Yes, ghosts have always been popular, one way or another. This book aims to serve as a guide to the many different types. Since ghosts are found around the world, this is very much a "field guide" that can be carried with you. Whether you are close to home, on a Civil War battlefield, or in a foreign country, dip into this guide and learn all you can about your surroundings. It is said that we are only afraid of the unknown—of those things with which we are not familiar. The more we learn about a subject, the less afraid we become. So read, learn, and enjoy your ghosts!

Ancestral Ghosts

As the name implies, ancestral ghosts are the spirits of departed family members. There are various reasons for ghosts to haunt the living world. It may be that they are drawn to a particular area through a traumatic experience they had there (possibly the manner of their death) or through experiencing great happiness in that location. There can also be the need to contact the living, either to give a message or simply to let the survivors know that the spirit is still in existence, albeit on another plane. Many times the spirit is drawn back because of remorse for some actions or treatment of a relative or close friend.

Ancestral ghosts may watch over a new child and watch it grow and develop. They may be in attendance at weddings and other important events in the lives of surviving relatives. Deceased parents and grandparents have been seen in photographs of such events, materializing to be a part of them.

Japanese Ghosts

In the Japanese religion of Shintoism, deceased ancestors acquire the power of deities with supernatural attributes. Surviving relatives worship them by honoring their pictures, burning incense, and making offerings of food and drink. In this way, the ancestors are propitiated and will bring good luck to the family. They do have the potential for good or for evil, and their focus is on the same interests they held when alive. To the Japanese, the dead are no less than the living, taking part in the daily life of the family.

There are stories of ghosts of the ancestors materializing and remaining visible for years. For three days in July, there is the Festival of the Dead, at which time the deceased may return from the spirit world to look around at the country and to visit with the family. New mats are placed at all the family shrines, and fresh food is prepared and laid out ready for the ghosts' return. Some Shinto sects perform a rite in which a person is selected to be possessed by an ancestral spirit. It is believed that then, with the spirit acting through the living person, healings may be performed and prophecies made.

Traditional ghosts are the *Yurei*, which hang around after death mainly to seek vengeance for something that happened in life. Many of them are female. The name means "faint/dim/hazy spirit." The normal, non-vindictive spirit is the *Reikon*, which simply leaves the physical body and joins the other ancestors. Then there are the *Yokai*, or "bewitching apparitions." These always appear at dawn or dusk and include monsters and spirits like goblins. It's said that they sometimes steal small children. The *Obake* or *Bakemono* are general terms for preternatural beings of any sort and include the *Yurei* and *Yokai* but can also include anything strange and unusual.

In recent years, many ghosts have appeared in otherwise ordinary family photographs. These usually are seen as extra faces or—in a large number of cases—extra hands in the picture. There have also been sightings in Japanese videos. For example, an amateur video taken of a girl on a moving train, when slowed, showed a partially transparent figure of a girl outside the window. The sighting was at a section of track where more than one person had committed suicide by jumping from the train.

Shinrei Shashin is a phrase used to describe photos where ghosts or spirits decide to show all or part of themselves when a photo is taken. *Shinrei Shashin* is a popular subject on Japanese TV.

Ka

Ka (sometimes *ba*) is the name given to the ancient Egyptian spirit or soul or, more correctly, to a "double" of that soul, similar to an astral body. It has been referred to as an alter ego or guardian spirit. Not only humans but animals and even inanimate objects had kas. At the tomb of a deceased person, there would be built a "House of Ka"—a home for the double. The actual soul would make periodic visits to its counterpart at that house. The House of Ka is where offerings of food and drink would be left. If there was neglect, then the ka would be forced to leave that house and roam, as a ghost, eating and drinking whatever could be found. Such a ghost might be encountered by the living.

Revenant

The word *revenant* is sometimes used interchangeably with *ghost*. Revenants may be human or animal. "Revenant" covers the whole gamut of ghosts, apparitions, specters, poltergeists, phantoms, and so on. The word is from the French *revenir*, meaning "to return."

Animal Ghosts

Animals have spirits/souls, and they do go on to the after-life, just as humans do. Consequently, it's not unusual for some of those spirits to return—again as with humans— in ghostly form. Animals of all types have been seen as ghosts in a wide variety of locations. Not all reports of animal ghosts are sightings, however; some are sounds, such as animal footsteps on a tile floor, or a cat's meow or a dog's bark. Deceased family pets show up in snap-shots of family members, reuniting with their loved ones. For example, when Lady Hehir was photographed with her Irish wolfhound Tara, in 1926, there in the picture, behind Tara's rear end, was the face of Kathal, a Cairn terrier pet who had died six weeks before the photo-graph was taken. Kathal and Tara had been inseparable friends before the terrier's demise.

Similarly, a family photograph of two ladies and their maid at tea, taken in Tingewick, England, in 1916 shows a dark-colored dog standing beside one of the ladies. The photograph was taken by a retired CID (Secret Service) inspector. No one—photographer or sitters—saw anything of a dog there at the time. The dog is partially transparent in the photo.

Another family group picture, taken at Clarens, Switzerland, in August 1925, is of a mother with her baby in a carriage and a young son standing beside the carriage holding a toy kitten. But also visible in the picture, peeking around the toy, is the head of a real white kitten—one that had belonged to the family but that had died some weeks earlier.

In Real Ghosts, Restless Spirits, and Haunted Places,[2] Brad Steiger recounts the story of a ten-year-old boy whose pet dog had been run over and killed by a car, in late October 1971. Six or eight months later, the boy was playing a game of hide-and-seek with his friends, in a two-acre field of waist-high wild wheat. As he ran through the field, looking for his friends, the boy almost tripped over a dog. It was his deceased pet, Snoopy, who stood wagging his tail. The dog had very distinctive markings, and there was no mistaking him. The boy chased after the animal as it turned and trotted off through the wheat, disappearing from sight. The boy ran forward and suddenly came upon the cement block that he and his mother had placed in the field in lieu of a tombstone.

[2] Detroit: Visible Ink Press, 2003.

It still bore the name Snoopy, together with the date of death, written in permanent marker by the boy's mother.

Ghosts of horses, ponies, cattle, wild cats, and other animals have been seen. The sounds of deceased animals—including the raucous voice of a long-dead parrot—have also been heard.

Galleytrot

Also known as Black Shuck, or Old Shuck, the Galleytrot is a very large ghostly dog that appears in different parts of southern England as a harbinger of death. The dog's howls are usually heard before he is seen, and he is mostly seen prowling around graveyards or loping along lonely country roads. It is said that to meet or even catch a glimpse of the Galleytrot means that you or someone close to you will die within the year.

The Galleytrot is also known by such names as the Black Dog, Hellbeast, Churchyard Dog, and similar. In New England, especially in New Hampshire, there is a similar ghostly demon dog known as Ol' Doofus. Such "Hounds of the Devil" are also known in other parts of the world, and such a one was supposedly the inspiration for Sir Arthur Conan Doyle's tale *The Hound of the Baskervilles.* Whole packs of such spectral beasts can be found in folklore, such as the hounds associated with the Wild Hunt in Norse and Teutonic mythology. (*See also* **Whisht Hounds.**)

 Gef

Strange animal noises were heard in the farmhouse of James and Margaret Irving in September 1931. The farmhouse was known as Cashen's Gap and was located on the Isle of Man (in the middle of the Irish Sea) near the hamlet of Dalby. The noises came from the attic. The Irvings' thirteen-year-old daughter, Voirrey, soon discovered that the unseen animal could repeat words that she spoke. It later became a very fluent speaker. The animal told them that its name was Gef and that it came from New Delhi, India; it had been born there June 7, 1852. It did not say how it came to be in the attic of the farmhouse. It later earned the nickname "The Dalby Spook."

Supposedly, Gef spied on neighbors' activities and reported then to the Irving family. When word of this got around, the neighbors were very annoyed. James Irving kept diaries on all these activities from 1932 till 1935. These reports are presently in the Senate House Library, in the Harry Price archives.

Journalists gathered to try to catch a glimpse of Gef, but failed. Many said it was a ghost or phantom, or just a product of the Irvings' imaginations. There was some poltergeist activity that seemed to center around the daughter Voirrey. Both ghost hunter Harry Price and Dr. Nandor Fodor (International Institute for Psychical Research) investigated the episode but could find no evidence of fraud.

In 1937 the Irvings moved away, and ten years later the farmer who bought the land saw a strange creature and shot it. It turned out to be a mongoose.

⌒⌒⌒∘ Ghost Horses ∘⌒⌒⌒

The Pony Express was in existence between April 1860 and October 1861. This rapid mail service that operated between St. Joseph, Missouri, and Sacramento, California. One of the old Pony Express stations still standing is Hollenberg Station in Kansas. Hollenberg's administrator, Duane Durst, has many times heard the sound of footsteps on the second floor and of furniture being moved, although he knows that the upper floor is completely empty. But he and others have also heard the sounds of horses whinnying and stamping. Late at night there has been heard the creaking of saddles and the pounding of hooves, as of ponies galloping past. "When the wind blows," says Durst, "you hear a lot of creaking and groaning, and the sounds of someone upstairs."

Whisht Hounds

Seen in the southwest of England, in Devon and Cornwall, the Whisht Hounds are a ghostly pack of dogs associated with the old pagan deity Woden (Odin of Norse mythology). They are said to be black with red eyes, though at times they may appear headless. As a pack, they follow a figure on horseback who is sup-posedly the Devil, Woden, or even Sir Francis Drake, depending upon local legend. (Drake lived in the seven-hundred-year-old Buckland Abbey, Devon—itself a haunted building.) As with the Galleytrot, it is said that to sight the Whisht Hounds means death within the year. Many country folk, even today, claim that they have heard the baying of the hounds, usually "over in the next valley," and have hurried home very much afraid.

Midsummer's Eve is the prime time for a sighting of the Whisht Hounds, though they may appear at any time of the year, usually in the dark of the moon. (*See also* **Galleytrot.**)

Wild Hunt

The Wild Hunt is the name given to the ghostly appearance of men, horses, and hounds that, on stormy nights, roam the countryside of southwestern England. It is also known generally across northern and western Europe, especially in northern Germany. The procession may be seen in particular at *Samhain,* or Hallowe'en. The leader of the hunt has been described as young, old, male, and female, by various observers, and has been named Herne the Hunter, Woden, Satan, Holda, Valdemar Atterdag, Bertha, and even Diana or Hecate.

Sometimes the hunt takes place across the sky, rather than on the ground, and may be attributed to violent thunderstorms. At various times, and in various places, it has been said that the purpose of the hunt is to seek out sinners or the unbaptized and to take them to Hell. If in danger of viewing the hunters, you should fall to the ground and cover your face. Some say that you also need to recite the Lord's Prayer. The hunt has been reported as seen in England as recently as the late twentieth century.

Apparitions

An apparition is a ghost sighting or sensing—the super-normal perception of the spirit of a deceased person or animal. Yet apparitions are of a wide variety of types. They may seem transparent or they may appear solid; they may be complete or only partially visible; they may seem to communicate vocally or be mute; they may be helpful or threatening. Some apparitions are no more than "memories" of the deceased, in effect replaying the events (of the person's death, perhaps) like the repeated playing of a DVD.

Some apparitions are of the living. They might be the astral body of someone alive but located elsewhere that has suddenly become visible to the observer. Some people with strong psychic ability are able to see astral bodies on occasion.

What are known as "crisis apparitions" are those
astral bodies that appear to loved ones at a moment of
crisis—just as they are being killed or are dying, for
example. There have been countless examples of this,
especially during wartime, with sons and daughters,
husbands and wives, appearing to their loved ones at
the moment of death. This is frequently the astral body
being seen, which appears in the brief moments before
the actual death and then becomes the true apparition as
the death takes place. Such crisis apparitions generally
appear in the viewer's everyday surroundings. Crisis ap-
paritions may also appear as a warning to the observer,
or to direct them to a particular locale.

 Airmen

A hotel was made out of the old World War II Officers'
Mess at Bircham Newton Airfield, England. The hotel
was for a construction industry training company, and one
part of the building was for making training films. Behind
the building, a double squash court was erected, and it
soon became apparent that one of these squash courts
was haunted by an airman. The ghost was spotted by two
squash players who then set up a tape recorder where they
had seen the apparition. When they played back the tape
the following morning, they heard the sounds of a busy
airfield—male and female voices, aircraft taking off and
landing, machinery, unusual "pinging" noises, and what
they described as "strange unearthly groaning noises."

Ghostly airmen were seen by a number of people; one of the apparitions was seen to walk through a brick wall that had not been there when the airfield was originally in use. A BBC reporter who spent a night there reported feelings of "intense cold," hearing doors banging, and the complete breakdown of previously flawless recording equipment.

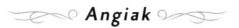

Angiak

According to Inuit folklore, if a child is deliberately killed by being left exposed in the snow, its ghost—known as an *angiak*—will repeatedly appear to the parents and other members of the tribe unless the tribe moves away from the site as soon as possible after the death. It is said that the baby's wailing cries can be heard, haunting the tribe.

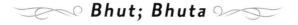

Bhut; Bhuta

This is Hindu and is considered to be an evil ghost, one that is usually associated with a suicide, someone who was executed, or someone who died by accident. It is said that *bhut*s have no shadows and that they never rest on the ground. To avoid meeting one, then, it is recommended to lie on the ground. A good way to protect yourself from encountering a bhut is to burn tumeric, which they detest.

Bourru

Of unknown origin, the *bourru* is the apparition of a figure dressed as a monk. It is said to walk the streets of Paris, France, late at night. It will look in at the windows of timid people, often passing back and forth a number of times to do so. Unruly children are often told that the bourru will come to get them if they do not behave.

Churel

In India, the *churel* is the ghost of a woman who has died in childbirth, or in a state of ceremonial impurity. Originally it was the ghost of a person of low caste in India. The ghost is regarded as malignant. It has no mouth and shuffles along on feet that are reversed. Sometimes the churel appears in the form of a beautiful woman, to attract and trap young men and to then keep them in its power until they are old and gray. Many times a woman who dies in childbirth will be buried face down to prevent the spirit from becoming a churel.

Crisis Apparitions

Mrs. Violet Almond's husband was in the army, fighting on the battlefield in North Africa in December 1943. Mrs. Almond awoke one night to see an apparition of her husband who was being shelled and was praying that he be saved so that he could see his wife again. She later learned, upon his safe return, that he had been doing exactly that on the day in question.

On the morning of March 14, 1928, an RAF officer named G. L. P. Henderson awoke in his cabin on board the ship *Barrabool,* south of the Canary Islands en route for England. He saw an apparition of his longtime friend Captain W. G. R. Hinchcliffe standing in the cabin. Hinchcliffe was obviously in distress, repeating over and over, "What am I going to do? I've got this woman with me and I'm lost. I'm lost!" Then the apparition faded away. At the time, Hinchcliffe was attempting to cross the Atlantic in a 32-foot Stinson Detroiter monoplane. His copilot was the Honorable Elsie McKay, a British heiress. Three days later, Henderson received word that Captain Hinchcliffe and Miss McKay were missing.

Mrs. Paquet awoke one morning, in Chicago, feeling very anxious about her brother Edmund, who worked on a tugboat in the harbor. She couldn't get rid of the feeling and got up to make herself a cup of tea. As she turned from the pantry, she saw an apparition of her brother standing with his back to her. He seemed to be in the act of falling forward and she could see that his legs had become entangled in a coil of rope. He seemed to disappear over a small railing. She knew instantly that her brother had drowned. Much later, she received word that indeed he had, under the very circumstances she had seen in the vision.

Crisis apparitions of a slightly different type were those that came about through the crash of Eastern Airlines Flight 401, in the Florida Everglades outside Miami on December 29, 1972. The landing gear of the Lockheed L-1011 malfunctioned, and, with the crew distracted, the plane crashed in the Everglades, killing 101 people. Captain Robert Loft, the pilot, and Flight Engineer Don Repo were among the dead. For some time after that, airline personnel reported sightings of Bob Loft and Don Repo. One flight engineer reported finding Repo at his seat on another airplane preparing for takeoff. The very live-seeming ghost said, "I've already done the preflight check." Then he faded away to nothing! On another flight, preparing for takeoff from New York, a flight captain and two attendants reported seeing Bob Loft in the airplane's first class section. They briefly spoke with him before he, too, vanished.

Deathbed Visions

There have been many recorded instances of what are termed "deathbed visions"—when the person dying sees the spirits of already deceased loved ones standing waiting to escort him or her through the transition we call death. On rare occasions, the person sitting with the dying man or woman will also see the apparition of the spirit who has arrived.

Headless Horseman

The best-known headless horseman is from Washington Irving's 1820 fictional tale *The Legend of Sleepy Hollow*, in which the lean and lanky schoolmaster Ichabod Crane competes with "Brom Bones" Van Brunt for the hand of Katrina Van Tassel, the only daughter of a wealthy farmer. A headless horseman—supposedly the ghost of a Hessian trooper who lost his head to a cannonball—chases Ichabod when he departs a party late one night. Ichabod keeps running and thus leaves the field clear for Van Brunt. There are many parallels between Irving's tale and the 1790 poem by Robert Burns, "Tam O'Shanter."

In 1902, at the Gothic-style Woodchester Mansion in Gloucestershire, England, the local vicar reported seeing various apparitions, including that of a headless horseman, in the driveway of the mansion.

In Santa Fe, New Mexico, hauntings are reported at the La Posada Hotel on East Palace Avenue, the Laguna Pueblo Mission, the Grant Corner Inn, the Church of San Miguel, La Fonda Hotel, and the Legal Tender Restaurant and Saloon located in the central part of town. In addition, a phantom headless horseman is reported to roam Alto Street, riding down to the Santa Fe River.

A French silver prospector's ghost reportedly haunts Twin Sisters' Hollow, South of Ole Bull's Castle at Cross Fork, Pennsylvania. In the early 1700s, the prospector encountered Native Americans who killed him and lopped off his head. Under an October full moon, his headless body can still be seen riding, head tucked under his arm.

The apparition of a headless horseman has been sighted riding from Bandera, Texas, to Center Point, Texas. Supposedly he was a mail carrier who lost his head to Apaches in the 1800s. And there have been sightings of a ghost wagon full of settlers who were massacred by the Apaches.

Also in Texas, in 1850 a Texas Ranger named Creed Taylor tracked down a rustler named Vidal, who had stolen some of Taylor's prize mustangs. Taylor decapitated Vidal and tied his body to the back of a wild mustang, his hands fastened to the pommel. The horse was let loose to wander the area as a warning to other would-be rustlers. So began the legend of *El Muerto* ("The Headless One"), who was seen by many for years after. Soldiers at Fort Inge (today's Uvalde) began to see the headless rider. Travelers and ranchers in "No Man's Land" also reported continuing to see the apparition. It was reported as having been seen near Freer, Texas, in 1969.

La Llorona

La Llorona is "The Weeper" or "The Weeping Woman" in Mexican folklore. It is the ghost of a mother who is searching for her murdered child. There are countless explanations of the origins of the story . . . from Aztec mythology through vampire legends to modern superstition. Although a Mexican-based story, the apparition has been seen in the United States as far north as Indiana, and in all states south of there. She is most frequently encountered as a hitchhiker, standing inexplicably on a long stretch of uninhabited highway, where she tells the story of her search for her child and then vanishes. She may be seen as a hitchhiker at the side of the road (or even in the very middle of the road) and be picked up, or she may suddenly appear inside the moving car. She is variously described as beautiful and seductive or as old and unattractive. She wears either a white dress or a black one. She has long black hair and very long fingernails. She usually appears to men who are driving alone.

Pele

See **Religious Ghosts**

Wraith

The appearance of a wraith is supposedly an omen of death. It is frequently thought to be the double of a living person (*see* **Doppelgänger,** *page 114*). In that sense, it is seen immediately before and/or after the person's death. Some say that the wraith is vengeful and will harm all those it meets, though this is not a universal belief. The classical depiction of a wraith is of a tall gaunt figure in a black cloak or white shroud, sometimes with a skull for a face and at other times with no face visible, and with a long, thin, or bony hand extended.

Battlefield Ghosts

Battlefields, with the usually vast number of deaths in-
volved, are common places to see ghosts. Such deaths are
invariably traumatic and thus support the idea of spirits
of the deceased remaining at the scene.

In addition to those discussed here, haunted battle-
fields in America include Antietam, Maryland; Chicka-
mauga, Tennessee; The Alamo, San Antonio, Texas;
USS Arizona, Pearl Harbor, Oahu, Hawaii; Chalmette
National Battlefield and Cemetery, Louisiana; and Cold
Harbor, Richmond, Virginia.

Fredericksburg, Virginia

Fredericksburg was George Washington's hometown,
and there are many reports of hauntings throughout

the area, in houses, in the Rising Sun Tavern (built by George Washington's brother Charles), and throughout the surrounding area. Civil War soldiers, Indian maidens, and even the voice of Thomas Jefferson have drawn ghost hunters to Fredericksburg.

But it was the Civil War battles that prompted most of the ethereal activity. For nearly a month before the start of the engagement, Confederate and Union troops gathered around the city. Then, on December 12, 1862, Union forces crossed the Potomac and entered the town. This was the start of one of the Civil War's bloodiest battles, resulting in more than 17,000 casualties.

There are four battlefields in the one area: Fredericksburg, the Wilderness, Chancellorsville, and the Spotsylvania Court House. Many ghosts have been seen—mostly wounded soldiers, soldiers standing guard duty, soldiers marching. Ghost lights have also been in evidence.

Gettysburg, Pennsylvania

The battlefield at Gettysburg is an interesting story. Certainly, with 620,000 soldiers dying in that conflict, there is plenty of room for apparitions of the dead. One such encounter took place in the 1990s, close to an area known as Devil's Den, a jumble of boulders near the Emmitsburg Road. There are cannons at a place with a plaque to the "Maelstrom of Death." One dark night, an amateur ghost hunter was standing by the cannon when he heard footsteps. Then he and his companion heard what sounded like soldiers running on hard ground, even though the area was covered with dense brush. Shortly after that, they heard what they imagined to be a wounded horse, snorting and panting as it closed in on them. Then, suddenly, everything was still and quiet—no further sounds.

In 1981 two reenactors, dressed in Union uniforms they hoped were as authentic in their detail as they could be, were resting after the day's strenuous mock battle "fighting." They were on Little Round Top, gazing down at the valley between there and Houck's Ridge. Suddenly they saw a Federal soldier emerge from some bushes and start up the slope toward them. He seemed weary, and his uniform and his face were sweat-stained and begrimed with the smoke and dirt of battle. When he got to them, he spoke a few words and handed them two rounds of ammunition. Although it was forbidden to carry live rounds during the reenactment, these two cartridges were authentic to the point of containing the mini balls found in the real rounds. He turned and went back the way he had come, eventually disappearing from sight. The two rounds turned out to be authentic ammunition from the period. There was no further sign of the soldier.

~~~○ Little Big Horn, ○~~~ Montana

On June 25, 1876, General George Armstrong Custer led six hundred soldiers of the Seventh Cavalry Regiment in a battle against the Native American Sioux Nation headed by Sitting Bull and Crazy Horse. It was the Battle of Little Bighorn in Montana. Custer himself, together with 265 soldiers, met their deaths. There have been many reports of the return of various spirits—both military and Native American—to that site.

Virtually all psychics who visit the site of Little Bighorn are immediately aware of the tremendous sadness that seems to hang in the air. This is especially strong at Last Stand Hill. Many of the Battlefield Cemetery employees have reported phenomena at the Stone House, the two-story building for the park's staff. Phantoms have appeared at the foot of beds, ghost lights have been seen, footsteps have been heard. The ghost of Custer himself has been seen by a number of people at the Battlefield Museum.

The ghost of Second Lieutenant Benjamin Hodgson has been seen repeatedly where he fell and was killed, on a steep hill, but he is far from the only ghost that appears regularly. Most such appearances seem to occur on the anniversary of the massacre: June 25. The Visitor Center is also haunted by an unidentified soldier.

Mons, France

Gettysburg, Little Big Horn, Valley Forge, Fredericksburg, and similar sites have their stories of ghostly sightings, but the most legendary story concerns the supposed mass sightings of a host of ghostly figures filling the skies during the World War I at the Battle of Mons, in France. This was the first major engagement of the British Expeditionary Force against overwhelming numbers of German troops. Despite being so outnumbered, the British forces acquitted themselves well, though they had to retreat as fast as possible. It was subsequently reported that the skies that night were filled with apparitions of either angels (depending upon who was telling the tale) or English bowmen led by none other than England's patron saint, Saint George.

The British Spiritualist magazine, *Spiritualist*, carried the story on April 24, 1915—some eight months after the event. It seems, however, that what was reported as having been seen in the sky was heavily weighted by a fictional story titled *The Bowmen*, by Arthur Machen, a Welsh author. Machen later did his best to point out the facts of the case, but despite his efforts churches across Britain endorsed sermons about "Divine Providence on the side of the British" in the war. It seems possible that some few people did think they saw angelic forces in the sky on the night of the battle, but there is no documented supporting evidence.

Roman Army

Although not on a battlefield, a contingent of Roman soldiers has put in an appearance in York, England, at the Treasurer's House. In 1953, a young man named Harry Martindale—an apprentice plumber—was working in the cellar of the mansion when he heard what he described as a musical note, like a horn being blown. Suddenly a Roman soldier stepped out through the wall of the cellar and, followed by a legion of men, marched on and disappeared on the far side. The original Roman road that once ran through that area had been at a slightly lower level, so Harry's view of the soldiers was of them with the lower extremities of their legs hidden below the floor. Some were on horseback, and the lower parts of the horses' legs were also hidden.

The young man was understandably terrified and ran to crouch down in a corner of the room while they all marched through. He was later found there by the museum curator. The curator could believe his story since he had himself witnessed such an apparition just a few years before.

∾ Valley Forge, ∿ Pennsylvania

Although there seem to be few actual graves at Valley Forge, there have been many reports of ghostly sightings, with spectral figures of soldiers and the sounds of men moaning in agony. No actual battle was fought there, except the battle with the elements through the winter of 1777–78. Valley Forge is close to Philadelphia, Pennsylvania, and was where General Washington and the Continental Army camped for six months.

Near the sites known as Varnum's and Huntington's Quarters, there appear to be a number of what could be unmarked graves. Others may be along the Outer Line Drive going down toward Wayne's Woods. However, there are few references to Valley Forge burials found in eighteenth-century documents.

In the nearby Phoenixville Public Library there have been reports—vouched for by the library director—of strange lights and of books falling off shelves, but these seem unrelated to the military events at Valley Forge.

Biblical Ghosts

The Bible is full of references to materializations, apparitions, and spirit contact. They can be found in Genesis 18:1, 28:11–19; 32:24; Exodus 24:10, 24:11; Samuel 28; Ezekiel 10, 11; Daniel 5:5; Matthew 14:25–27; Luke 24:15, 16, 29–31; John 20:12, 14, 19, 26.

As a brief example, in Daniel 5:5 it says, "In the same hour came forth fingers of a man's hand, and wrote over against the candlestick upon the plaster of the wall of the king's palace: and the king saw the part of the hand that wrote"—a wonderful description of a partial materialization such as reported at many Spiritualist séances of the late nineteenth and early twentieth centuries. Another example, from Luke: "And it came to pass, as he sat at meat with them, he took bread and blessed it, and brake, and gave it to them. And their eyes were opened,

and they knew him; and he vanished out of their sight."
Again, a typical dematerialization.

John 20:19 describes an event that is supposed to
have taken place two days after the crucifixion, which
was carried out on the Jewish Sabbath. This is described
as being on "the first day of the week." Jesus, early in the
day, had appeared to Mary Magdalene in the garden of
the sepulcher and told her to fetch his brethren. When
they had assembled in a room, with the door closed "for
fear of the Jews," Jesus materialized before them. Apparently it was a solid materialization, for he showed them
his hands and side, to verify who he was. Later, he disappeared, only to show up again to the disciples at the Sea
of Tiberias.

Perhaps the best-known example of materialization
of a deceased spirit detailed in the Bible is the case of Saul
and the "woman of Endor" (not a "witch" in the original,
but merely "a woman that hath a familiar spirit"—basi-
cally a Spiritualist medium). In I Samuel 28 there is the
story of Saul's visit to the woman and his request to meet
with the departed spirit of Samuel. The Bible states that
"Samuel was dead, and all Israel had lamented him, and
buried him in Ramah." Yet Saul needed his advice and so
talked the Endor woman into causing him to materialize,
which she did.

Celebrity Ghosts

As will be seen, many celebrities become ghosts on their demise. Why this should be so we do not know. It may have something to do with the focus of attention that has been directed at them for a lengthy period. Perhaps the spirit is loath to give up that spotlight? In some cases, however, it is the manner of death that accounts for the reappearance after death. As has been shown (See **Crisis Apparitions** *and* **Battlefield Ghosts,** *page 33), trauma may contribute to the lingering of the spirit.*

Lucille Ball

Lucille Ball died in 1969, at age seventy-seven. She had lived at 100 North Roxbury Drive, in Beverly Hills, and there have been reports that she's still there . . . as a ghost. Objects, including large items of furniture, are moved about the room when no one is present. Voices—hers being easily recognizable—are heard coming from the empty attic. Windows are opened and closed; doors are locked and unlocked. Windows have also been broken. All of this may be due to the fact that the house was virtually rebuilt after Lucille's death, with walls taken out and the whole floor plan rearranged.

James Dean

Since James Dean died such a violent death (in a head-on car crash between his Porsche 550 Spyder and a 1950 Ford Tudor), it's not surprising that his ghost hangs around. The accident occurred in September 1955 near the crossing of California State Routes 466 and 41, a few miles on from Blackwell's Corner. His ghost has been seen at the Fairmount Cemetery in Indiana, where his body lies, as well as at the site of the deadly crash.

Redd Foxx

The star of the popular television series *Sanford and Son* died of a heart attack in October 1991 on Stage 31 at Paramount Studios. His Las Vegas home, on Eastern Avenue and Rawhide Street, has changed hands a number of times, and each of the owners has claimed that the late comedian still appears there, usually playing pranks. The first owner of the house was plagued by a sliding glass door that would repeatedly open by itself, so he had it replaced. . . . The new door did the same thing! Another owner, who had a real estate business, reported that the computers would turn on and off by themselves and files would disappear.

Jean Harlow

Jean Harlow was the original "platinum blonde bombshell" of the silver screen in the 1920s and 1930s. Her brief career ended in 1937, at age twenty-six, when she died of kidney disease. She had lived at 1353 Club View Drive, Los Angeles, then at husband Paul Bern's mansion at 9820 Easton Drive, Beverly Hills. She left there when Bern committed suicide and moved to 512 North Palm Drive. Harlow's apparition has been seen on a number of occasions at the Easton Drive address and also at her original home on Club View Drive.

Jesse James

Jesse James's family farm was northeast of Kearney, Missouri. He was originally buried on the farm, but later reburied with his wife at Mount Olivet Cemetery. It seems his attachment is more for the old family homestead than it is for the final resting place of his bones, for his ghost is frequently seen at the farm. Lights are seen there at night and seem to move around; doors slam; and there is an overwhelming feeling of "otherworldly presence" picked up by numerous psychics and ghost hunters. A docent at the farm museum has reported hearing very distinct footsteps following her through the house and especially through Jesse's old bedroom. She described the footsteps as "the thump of boots." Others have heard muttered voices, seen furniture move, and seen vague misty shapes appear and move around. Jesse is also said to haunt the rooms of the Talbott Tavern in Bardstown, Kentucky—a favorite hangout of Jesse and his James-Younger gang.

John Lennon

John Lennon was shot to death at the Dakota Building, 1 West 72nd Street, New York, in 1980. (When alive, John claimed to have seen what he termed "The Crying Lady Ghost" in the building.) Since his death, John's ghost has been seen many times. In 1983, a musician named Harrow saw the figure in a Dakota entranceway. Amanda Moores, a writer who was with Harrow, also saw the apparition. Other people, including Yoko Ono, have seen Lennon inside the building.

Marilyn Monroe

Marilyn Monroe died of an overdose of sleeping pills on August 4, 1962, at a house in Brentwood. The Hollywood Roosevelt Hotel is a place she often stayed when at the height of her fame, and her ghost is said to haunt that place on a regular basis, as well as the Brentwood home. An apparition of her has also been seen at her grave, at Westwood Memorial Cemetery in Los Angeles, on Glendon Avenue.

Several people have also seen Marilyn's apparition at the Cal-Neva Lodge on Crystal Bay at Lake Tahoe. The lodge was owned, in 1960, by Frank Sinatra, and he and his longtime friend Marilyn often stayed there. She always stayed in cabin #3, close to a tunnel that was a secret passage during Prohibition. A security guard one time went to see if he could help a beautiful blonde woman who was standing in the tunnel, crying. As he approached her, she turned away and walked through the wall.

 Elvis Presley

Elvis Presley's ghost not only haunts Graceland, in Memphis, Tennessee (where he died in 1977), but also hangs around the Las Vegas Hilton, where he performed for so many years. His apparition has also been seen in a building off Nashville's Music Row, where Elvis recorded *Heartbreak Hotel*. Although the building is no longer a recording studio for RCA, it does house a television production studio. It's said that if anyone mentions Presley's name, all manner of strange things occur—lights blow out, ladders fall down, noises come onto the sound tracks.

A year after Presley's death, investigator Hans Holzer held a séance at the Drake Hotel in Manhattan, with Dee Presley, Elvis's stepmother. During the sitting, Elvis came through and, among other things, made jokes about Colonel Tom Parker.

George Reeves

Some say that George Reeves was frustrated at being typecast in his role of Superman, and that he became despondent enough to commit suicide, in 1959, just days before his planned marriage. However, all the evidence seems to point toward homicide, involving a jealous ex-lover, her even more jealous husband, and others who wanted Reeves dead.

It has been said that Reeves's ghost appears in his old bedroom in Benedict Canyon Drive, dressed in his Superman costume. He stays for a while and then gradually fades away to nothing. Certainly realtors did try to sell his house after his death, to settle his estate, but buyers always claimed they heard strange noises in the upstairs bedroom where George had been killed. On examination it would sometimes be found that the bedding had been ripped away, clothes were strewn about the floor, and there was an odor of gunpowder in the room. Buyers and tenants came and went rapidly, especially when they saw an apparition of Reeves.

There were police reports of flashing lights, of gunshots, and of strange noises; none of it could be explained. In the 1980s the house was being used for a television show and the cast and crew saw an apparition of Reeves, which appeared and then abruptly vanished. Such reports have continued through to the present.

Rudolph Valentino

Rudolph Valentino was a great believer in the occult and in spirit communication. Speaking of death, he once said, "Why call it Death? If we give it the name Death, why surround it with dark fears and sick imaginings? I am not afraid of the unknown." He died in 1926 at the age of thirty-one, from peritonitis, but he didn't leave his home. His ghost still haunts the grounds of Falcon Lair, 6776 Wedgewood Place, in the

Whitley Heights section of Beverly Hills. He has been seen in hallways, bedrooms, at a second-floor window, and in the stables. He has also been seen at his old beach house in Oxnard and at the Santa Maria Inn in Santa Maria. At the inn he frequently knocks on a door, and his phantom figure has been seen reclining on a bed. Valentino's ghost is extremely active, also being seen near his burial site at the Cathedral Mausoleum at Hollywood Forever Memorial Park and at various locations at Paramount Studios.

John Wayne

John Wayne spent many hours on his yacht *The Wild Goose*. He died just a month after he sold the boat. It was bought by a lawyer named Lynn Hutchins, who lived in Santa Monica. Hutchins claimed that he many times saw an apparition of Wayne on the boat, and others have also seen the ghost there. Beer glasses have rattled on the bar, and people have strongly sensed Wayne's presence.

Orson Welles

Orson Welles died in Hollywood in October 1985. There is a rumor that his ghost appears on occasions at the Sweet Lady Jane Bakery and Restaurant at 8360 Melrose Avenue. The bakery is on the site of the old Ma Maison restaurant, which was Welles's favorite place to eat. Someone once remarked that Welles ate at the restaurant so often that "he probably haunts the place." This may be the source of the ghost stories; however, some do claim that they have either seen him there or at least smelled his cigar smoke.

Deceiving Ghosts

There are numerous instances when it seems highly improbable that messages given by ghosts or spirits are all they seem to be. From all the evidence obtained through competent Spiritualist mediums, it seems that just because the boundary of life and death is passed, the resultant ghost does not immediately become honest and trustworthy. Many deceased spirits retain their sense of humor and even, in some cases, their unreliable dispositions. In other words, it's not unknown for a ghost to blatantly lie to the living! The Swedish philosopher and mystic Emmanuel Swedenborg (1688–1772) said, "When spirits begin to speak with man he must beware lest he believe them in any thing; for they say almost anything. Things are fabricated by them and they lie. If man then listens and believes, they press on and deceive and seduce in divers ways."

Ghosts have been known to pass on information that has proven beneficial to the receiver. The location of misplaced wills and other important documents is a good example. But anything that cannot be verified should never be accepted at face value.

With this in mind, it should also be recognized that many ghosts are of departed spirits who either do not realize that they are dead or are unable to come to terms with that fact. They are, many times, simply lonely and want to retain connection with the physical world. They may, then, say or indicate just about anything that they feel will keep them in contact with the observer, stretching the truth or lying outright just to hold the attention.

 Alu-Demon

This is a Semitic (belonging to a language family originating in southwestern Asia) entity that is said to be the female offspring resulting from union between a succubus and a human. It hides itself in caves and around dark corners and slinks through darkened streets at dead of night, laying in wait for the unwary. It is said that the *Alu-Demon* has been known to enter bedrooms and to terrorize the people there, threatening to pounce upon them if they try to close their eyes. It will freely answer questions, but the answers it gives are unreliable and often unintelligible. Though part demon, not all Alu-Demons are inherently evil (though those of a good disposition are extremely rare). The typical Alu-Demon is said to have dark eyes and hair, with small black horns projecting just above the eyes. They also have small, leathery, black wings.

Fairies

There are many definitions of fairies—also various spellings: fairy, faerie, fayerye, fayre, fay, fey, fae, and so on—relating to a type of nature spirit. The name comes from the Latin fata, *meaning "enchanted" or "bewitched." Fairies are often associated with ethereal beings of various mythologies. They are seen as counterparts to humans among the Teutonic races of Scandinavia, Germany, and Britain and among the Kelts of Ireland, Scotland, the Isle of Man, Wales, and Brittany. The Irish word is* sheehogue *or* sidheog, *a diminutive of* banshee *and, according to the* Book of Armagh, *fairies are the "Gods of the Earth."*

There is some controversy regarding the size of fairies. (In Ireland can be found the huge formorians, while in South Africa are the tiny abatwas.) Up until the mid-sixteenth century, fairies were thought to be close to human size. In 1555, at the witch trial of Joan Tyrrye, it was said of her that "at one time she met with one of the fairies, being a man, in the market of Taunton, having a white rod in his hand, and she came up to him thinking to make an acquaintance of him." Apparently Joan did not realize that the man was a fairy until he disappeared. In 1588 Alesoun Peirsoun of Fifeshire said, "A man in green appeared to me, a lusty man with many men and women with him." In the evidence presented at the witch trials, there were many instances of people meeting with fairies and not realizing that was what they were, there being no great difference in their size. In Shakespeare's Merry Wives of Windsor, the bard has a full-grown woman, Mistress Page, dress as a fairy and expect to be accepted as one. It was not until later that the concept of fairies as diminutive beings came about. This was first promoted by Edmund Spenser in his Faerie Queen and was later picked up by Shakespeare in (A Midsummer Night's Dream) and by others.

One belief is that fairies are spirits of the dead. There is an old tale of a man caught by the fairies who found that when he stared hard at one of them it changed into the likeness, or ghost, of a deceased neighbor of his. There are many folktales that are told, sometimes featuring fairies and sometimes with those same characters described as ghosts.

Abatwas

Abatwas are tiny creatures found in Zulu mythology. They are said to be able to hide under a leaf or even a blade of grass. The idea of abatwas comes from the African native spirit *Vash'Nok*, meaning "whose tears fell and burst." There is a correspondence with abatwas found in Yesso, Japan. There, dwarves were thought to live in semi-subterranean houses or "pit" dwellings. The Aino word meaning "pit dweller" is very similar to the word for a burdock leaf. Since the dwarves were known to be very small people, it wasn't long before they were thought of as being so small that they could hide under a burdock leaf!

Elf

Originally a creature from Germanic mythology, the elf (*Ælf*) is of a race of minor fertility and nature deities. The name means "white spirit" or "shining spirit." Known for their great beauty, elves are dwellers in the forest and guardians of the trees. They may—in some areas—also be found in caves and attached to wells and springs. They have little weight and are therefore able to walk on surfaces that would not support most creatures. There were variations on the name, such as *dunælfen*—hill dwellers—and *wyldælfen*—wild elves. The plant known as Enchanter's Nightshade (*Circæa lutetiana*) was used by Saxon leeches, or doctors, as an antidote for magic done by evil elves. In Scandinavian mythology, the home of the Light Elves is *Álfheim*.

Formorian

These are hideous monsters that originally inhabited Ireland, according to folklore. They were the early gods preceding the Tuatha Dé Dannan, or "peoples of the goddess Danu," who were a race of people found in Irish mythology thought to derive from the pre-Christian gods of Ireland. According to an eleventh-century text, *Lebor na hUidre* ("The Book of the Dun Cow"), the *formorians* had the body of a man and the head of a goat. It was also said that they had one eye, one arm, and one leg. They could often be heard from a distance, making a great booming noise. They were sometimes referred to as "Mickleton Hooters."

Goblin

See **Spirits**

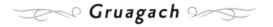

Gruagach

From the Gaelic *gruag,* meaning "wig," this is described as "the long-haired one." It is a male or female fairy, with long hair, who is protective of humans. Often seen as the ghost of a relative or neighbor, the *gruagach* is associated with cattle. In Scotland, milk was always put out for this fairy so that it would watch over the cattle through the night. If no milk was set aside for it, then the cattle would produce no milk the following morning. Sometimes classed with brownies, the gruagach seems to work mainly with cattle, while brownies are general house spirits.

Hobgoblin

A mischievous ghost who dresses in brown or green leather (though sometimes runs around naked). Generally friendly and helpful but with a wicked sense of humor. They are looked upon as hearth spirits and are found throughout England and Scotland. They favor farmhouses rather than town and city dwellings. They especially like dairy farms, and they love warm fires. Once a hobgoblin decides to take up residence, it's very difficult to get rid of him.

Phi

A fairy found in Thailand. It runs through the forest, and if it encounters anyone, it will shake that person so hard that he or she becomes ill. The only cure is to lay the person under the tree they last rested under and to exorcise them, driving out the *Phi* spirit's magic. Phi were originally nature spirits who lived in the streams, trees, mountains, and valleys.

Puck
(Poake; Pouke)

A mischievous English fairy of the woods. Closely aligned with Robin Goodfellow; sometimes the names are used interchangeably. Puck can shape-shift (assume other shapes and forms), a favorite being the form of a horse. It is sometimes seen with the body of a young boy and the head of a goat or vice versa. In the English county of Worcestershire, a common complaint is that people find themselves in bogs and ditches and claim they were "Poake-led."

Robin Goodfellow

An English fairy known for playing tricks on people. He can transform into other shapes, for example, running between someone's legs in the form of a rabbit or a hare and tripping them. He is very good at leading people astray, into ditches and bogs, much as does Puck. Robin Goodfellow is a fairy of the hobgoblin type.

Guardian Ghosts

A guardian spirit is one that is a personal protective spirit. Some refer to it as an angel or guide. Some believe that the guardian is actually the ghost of an ancestor or deceased close friend who has taken it upon themselves to watch over the living. They are most often seen in dreams, though they can reveal themselves at any time. The guardian spirit is thought to have been present from the very moment of birth and stays until death, giving advice through the unconscious, or even the conscious, mind. Premonitions are attributed to this spirit.

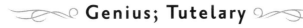

Genius; Tutelary

A genius, or tutelary, serves as a guardian who watches over and protects a person, a particular location, or even a whole nation. Athena, of the Greek pantheon, was such a deity, looking over the city of Athens. In Rome there were many such tutelaries, such as Levana, who specifically watched over children, and Diana of Aricia, who watched over the sacred grove at Aricia. Penates and Lares were local tutelaries. A personal guardian spirit was commonly called a genius.

Historic Ghosts

As the name implies, historic ghosts are those spirits that, when alive, were famous—or infamous—on the earth plane. Many monarchs fall into this category. Celebrity ghosts could also be classified as historic ghosts, though their fame may have been fleeting.

Abigail Adams

The story most often related about Abigail Adams is that when she and her husband, President John Adams, first moved into the White House (they were its first occupants), the structure was built mostly on a swamp.

Pennsylvania Avenue was unpaved and the house itself was unfinished. The main problem seemed to be—from Mrs. Adams's point of view—where to hang the laundry! She decided on the East Room as the warmest and driest. Today the ghost of Abigail Adams is most frequently seen in the East Room, or hurrying to or from it with her arms outstretched as though carrying a load of laundry. It is said that she can be easily recognized by the lace shawl and cap she favored in life. She is the oldest ghost to be encountered in the White House.

Anne Boleyn

Anne Boleyn was the second wife of England's King Henry VIII, supplanting Catherine of Aragon, who had been unable to provide Henry with a son and heir. When Anne herself failed to deliver a son, trumped-up charges of witchcraft, treason, incest, and adultery brought her to the Tower of London. She was beheaded. Ever since then, her ghost has been seen in various parts of the Tower and elsewhere.

She was beheaded on Tower Green, and this is one place she has been seen. Another is the White Tower, where since the mid-1800s she has been seen without her head (sometimes carrying the head). Soldier sentries have challenged her ghost, stabbed it ineffectually with

bayonets, and then fainted or run screaming from its sight. Her ghost has been seen leading a procession, singing, and also walking silently. Anne's ghost goes from the Queen's House to the Chapel of Saint Peter ad Vincula ("Saint Peter in Chains"). Inside the chapel, she walks down the aisle to her grave, which is underneath the altar. Her apparition has also been seen at Windsor Castle and at two of her childhood homes: Hever in Kent and Blicking Hall in Norfolk. At Blicking Hall, on the anniversary of her beheading, a spectral coach drives up to the entrance. Inside the coach sits Anne Boleyn with her head balanced on her lap. The coachman is also headless.

Catherine Howard

Another of King Henry VIII's wives—fifth of the six—was Catherine (or Katharine) Howard, whose ghost has also been seen at Hampton Court Palace. She has been seen running through the rooms and corridors of the palace. Her ghost has been seen at the Tower of London, where she was imprisoned when charged with adultery. Catherine was the first cousin of Anne Boleyn.

King Henry VIII

King Henry VIII's apparition has been seen at the Deanery Cloisters in Windsor Castle. People have not only seen him but have also heard his groans.

Abe Lincoln

Abraham Lincoln's ghost has been seen in a number of places, from where he was born to where he died and a great many locations in between. His apparition has been seen at the White House by many people, including Eleanor Roosevelt (though she *sensed* his presence rather than actually seeing him, as did Carl Sandburg), Mrs. Calvin Coolidge, Queen Wilhelmina of the Netherlands, Winston Churchill, a young clerk in the Roosevelt White House, and Presidents Franklin Delano Roosevelt, Herbert Hoover, and Harry S. Truman, though they all heard him rather than saw him. Maureen Reagan and her husband saw a transparent version of the ghost several times in the Lincoln bedroom.

Lincoln's grave site at Oak Ridge in Springfield, Illinois, has been the scene of some sightings, as has his childhood home there. Another place people claim to have seen him is Ford's Theater, the scene of his assassination.

Spirit photographer William H. Mumler (who died in 1884) was once visited by a "Mrs. Tyndall," a widow dressed in mourning, including a heavy veil. Her appointment had been set up by someone else, so Mumler had no way of knowing who she was. When the woman sat for the photograph, she put back her veil, revealing herself to be Mary Todd Lincoln, the president's widow. Mumler took the photograph, and when it was developed, it revealed the figure of the deceased president standing behind his wife. No one has ever been able to prove the photograph a fake.

 Mad Anthony

Nicknamed Mad Anthony by his troops because of his quick temper and his fearlessness, General Anthony Wayne was a major figure in the American Revolutionary War. He survived the war and died in Erie (then known as Fort Presque Isle), Pennsylvania, in 1796, on his way home from fighting Indians in Michigan. Thirteen years later, Wayne's son Isaac wanted to move the body back to the family cemetery in Chester County, Pennsylvania. The local Erie residents, however, wanted his body to stay where it was. Unknown to Isaac, local doctor James Wallace boiled the body and removed the flesh from the bones. The flesh and clothing were then buried in Erie and the bones given to Isaac to take home. Apparently the road back to Chester was rough, and on the way, some of the bones fell off the wagon and were lost. Isaac buried the rest of the body in the family plot at St. David's Cemetery. However, it is said that every New Year's morning, Mad Anthony's ghost rides the route (now U.S. 322) between Erie and Chester, looking for his missing bones.

Wayne's ghost has also been seen at Fort Ticonderoga (which he commanded in 1771), in a country house in Virginia, and on a mountain pass in northern New York State.

Dolley Madison

Dorothea Paine Madison was the wife of President James Madison. During the War of 1812, the White House was burned down, and the president and his wife moved temporarily into Colonel John Tayloe's "Octagon House." Dolley Madison's ghost has been seen there, as it has at Halcyon House and on the front porch of a house she lived in late in her life, in Lafayette Park. At the Octagon House, recent visitors have smelled the lilac perfume that Dolley Madison favored, even when they have not seen her ghost.

Gardeners were once ordered by the second Mrs. Woodrow Wilson to dig up the rose garden at the White House. The garden had been Dolley Madison's pride and joy. It's said that the gardeners stopped work and ran away when Dolley's ghost appeared to protect her garden.

Jane Seymour

Jane Seymour was the third wife of England's King Henry VIII. She died at Hampton Court Palace, giving birth to a son (who later became King Edward VI) in September 1537. It is said that Jane's ghost haunts Hampton Court, having been seen walking across one of the cobbled courtyards—the Clock Court—carrying a candle. She has also been seen in the Silver Stick Gallery there. Hampton Court, built by Cardinal

Thomas Wolsey and appropriated by King Henry, is ten miles west of central London.

Queen Elizabeth I

Queen Elizabeth I's ghost has been seen in the Royal Library at Windsor Castle, roaming from room to room.

In Elizabeth's day there was a well-known astrological physician named Simon Forman. He was satirized by Ben Jonson and laughed at by many, but he insisted that he once had a very erotic encounter with Queen Elizabeth. Most said it had to have been a dream, but Forman claims it was a real encounter with Elizabeth's ghost.

Screaming Skulls

There are a number of screaming skulls found in various locations around England—Appley Bridge, Lancashire; Bettiscombe Manor, Dorset; Turton Towers, Lancashire; Bowland Hall, Yorkshire; Brougham Hall, Cumbria; Old Timberbottom Farm, Bradshaw, Lancashire; Browsholme Hall, Lancashire; Burton Agnes Hall, Yorkshire; Old Prison, Bury St. Edmunds, Suffolk; Pack Horse Inn, Affetside, Lancashire; Higher Chilton Farm, Chilton Cantelo, Somerset; Fawkham Green, Kent; Warbleton Priory

Farm, Heathfield, Sussex; Flacgnallt Hall, Holywell, Wales; Ye Old White Hart Inn, Hull, Yorkshire; Calgarth Hall, Cumbria; Edward King's House, Lincoln; Flagg Hall, Derbyshire.

Typical of the stories connected with these skulls is the one found at Burton Agnes Hall in Yorkshire. The house was built in the seventeenth century by Sir Henry Griffith. One of his three daughters, Agnes, became very attached to the house. Agnes died when still young, after being attacked by footpads (low criminals who preyed on pedestrians) as she traveled home along the

Harpham Road. Before she died, she made her two sisters promise that they would bury her body in the family vault but would detach her head and keep that

in the house. This they did not do, and consequently the house became an ongoing scene of poltergeist activity, with slamming doors, rattling chains, screams, groans, and crashes. The local vicar recommended that the family fulfill Agnes's request, and the head was taken from the casket and placed in the house. The disturbances immediately ceased. But on two later occasions, the skull was taken back to the churchyard, to be put back in the family vault. Each time the poltergeist activity would begin again. Finally the skull was bricked up in one of the house walls, and all has remained quiet since.

Versailles Ghosts

On August 10, 1901, two young Englishwomen— Annie E. Moberly, daughter of the Bishop of Salisbury, and Eleanor M. Jourdain, daughter of a Derbyshire vicar—were visiting the Petit Trianon at Versailles, in France. In the words of Eleanor,

> We went on in the direction of the Petit Trianon but just before reaching what we knew to be the main entrance I saw a gate leading to a path cut deep below the level of the ground above, and as the way was open and had the look of an entrance that was used, I said "Shall we try this path? It must lead to the house," and we followed it. . . . I began to feel as if I were walking in my sleep; the heavy dreaminess was oppressive. At last we came upon a path crossing ours, and saw in front of us a building consisting of some columns roofed in, and set back in the trees. Seated on the steps was a man with a heavy black cloak round his shoulders, and wearing a slouch hat. At that moment the eerie feeling that had begun in the garden culminated in a definite impression of something uncanny and fear inspiring. The man slowly turned his face, which was marked by smallpox, his complexion was very dark. The expression was very evil and though I did not feel he was looking particularly at us, I felt a repugnance to going past him.

The two women went on to describe points of architecture and landscape that seemed to pinpoint the date of the building and its surrounds to around 1770, since alterations were later made to parts of the Petit

Trianon. In their perambulations, the ladies saw men in three-cornered hats, a woman with a large white hat, and others in the dress of the eighteenth century. The Petit Trianon was built by Louis XV for his mistress, the Marquise de Pompadour, who was later succeeded by Madame Du Barry. Later, Louis XVI gave the house to Marie Antoinette.

This would seem to be a fine case of clairvoyance, where the two women were acting as mediums and were able to see, and later describe in detail, events in a past century. However, it may also be that what they encountered were the ghosts of the people from that time.

Wild Edric

Wild Edric, or Eadric the Wild, was the nephew or grandson of Eadric Streona, Ealdorman of Mercia under Ethelred the Unready. He held extensive lands in Shropshire and other estates in Herefordshire. He refused to submit to the conquering Norman king William, in 1066, and led a number of rebellions against the invaders before finally submitting in 1070.

After fighting so fiercely and so consistently against the Normans, it was disappointing for the Saxons to see their hero give up and join the enemy. Because of this, he was condemned to haunt the borders of England and Wales, where he had fought for so many years. It is said that he lives on beneath the earth, with

his fairy wife Lady Godda (Goda or Gondul) and a band of faithful followers. They ride out whenever England is threatened and have been seen at the start of the Napoleonic Wars, Crimean War, World Wars I and II, and more recently the Falkland Islands conflict.

Inhuman Ghosts

Not just ghosts themselves but ghostly objects may appear
to people. In Chicago, near Bachelor's Grove Cemetery
(dubbed "the most haunted place in the world" by some),
off 143rd Street, there is a ghost house. Not a haunted
house, but a ghost house . . . sometimes it's there and
sometimes it's not! Apparently there are no records to
show that a house was ever at that site, yet many witnesses have seen it, sometimes on one side of the road and
sometimes on the other side. It always looks the same,
however—wooden columns, a porch swing, and dim
lights showing inside.

Ghost Airfield

In 1937, before the start World War II, young Victor Goddard (later to become Air Marshal Sir Victor Goddard) was flying his De Havilland Tiger Moth biplane across country when he spotted an airfield below him. He circled it and studied it, since it didn't appear on his charts. There were the usual hangars and many parked aircraft. When he returned to his own airfield, Goddard reported what he had seen, but no one could account for it. It wasn't until five years later that he again saw the place . . . shortly after it had been built. It was exactly where he had first seen the apparition of it and it was to become one of the main fighter stations in the Battle of Britain.

Ghost Airplane

A World War II heavy transport airplane has been seen on a number of occasions, by many different people, flying very low over Abergele in Wales. In 1987 a number of townspeople-witnesses said the plane was "rusty" and "very old," large and unmarked. They claimed it appeared "from nowhere," flew over them, and then vanished. Phone calls to RAF Valley, in Anglesey, and other airfields brought no information; no one knew of such an aircraft.

In Llangenyw, Denbighsire, Wales, mothers were picking up their children from school when the same "rusty" old WWII transport roared so low over their heads that they ducked down. The plane dipped into the valley and then clawed its way up and over the far hills and disappeared. Again, no authorities knew anything of it. The witnesses were told that no aircraft would ever be allowed to fly in that condition.

In 1994 the phantom airplane returned. This time the reports were from Wrexham. In the early evening of June 15, a couple driving over Denbigh Moors saw the aircraft suddenly appear in front of them. They estimated that it was only 100 feet off the ground and watched open-mouthed as it flew across in front of them, from left to right. It started to bank and turn to the right and then suddenly "vanished into thin air."

A father and his daughter were driving eastbound on the M62, in England, past Rishworth-Saddleworth Moor, when they saw a WWII Lancaster bomber, with smoke billowing from one of its engines, descending

rapidly. The father and daughter's car passed under the Scammonden Bridge, and when they came out the other side, there was no sign of the old airplane. No one knew anything of it.

Now little more than a collection of old huts, what was once Ridgewell (WWII) Airfield is where many locals have heard the sounds of piston engine aircraft, crashing planes, and shouting airmen. At Raydon—another WWII airfield in England—the ghost of a military policeman has been seen walking the area around the former Officers' Mess. There are also reports of phantom aircraft, including a P-47 and a B-17.

<s> Ghost Ships <s>

Ghost ships are ships that have been seen when it was known that that particular ship had sunk. The classic cases are of the *Flying Dutchman* and the *Mary* (not *Marie*) *Celeste,* though there are many more. According to legend, the *Flying Dutchman* is a ghost ship that is doomed to sail the seas forever. The sight of it (usually around the Cape of Good Hope, in bad weather) is supposedly a most unlucky omen, generally portending that the ship that spots it will itself sink. The first reference to the ship that appeared in print seems to be in George Barrington's *Voyage to Botany Bay* (1795):

> I had often heard of the superstition of sailors respecting apparitions, but had never given much credit to the report; it seems that some years since a Dutch man of war was lost off the Cape of Good Hope, and every soul on board perished; her consort weathered the gale, and arrived soon after at the Cape. Having refitted, and returning to Europe, they were assailed

by a violent tempest nearly in the same latitude. In the night watch some of the people saw, or imagined they saw, a vessel standing for them under a press of sail, as though she would run them down: one in particular affirmed it was the ship that had foundered in the former gale, and that it must certainly be her, or the apparition of her; but on its clearing up, the object, a dark thick cloud, disappeared. Nothing could do away the idea of this phenomenon on the minds of the sailors; and, on their relating the circumstances when they arrived in port, the story spread like wild-fire, and the supposed phantom was called the Flying Dutchman. From the Dutch the English seamen got the infatuation, and there are very few Indiamen, but what has some one on board, who pretends to have seen the apparition.

An article on the subject appeared in *Blackwood's* magazine for May 1821. In 1923 there was a sighting of it by a ship on its way to Australia from London by way of Cape Town. It was reported by Fourth Officer N. K. Stone:

About 0:15am we noticed a strange "light" on the port bow. . . . It was a very dark night, overcast, with no moon. We looked at this through binoculars and the ship's telescope, and made out what appeared to be the hull of a sailing ship, luminous, with two distinct masts carrying bare yards, also luminous; no sails were visible, but there was a luminous haze between the masts. There were no navigation lights, and she appeared to be coming close to us and at the same speed as ourselves. When first sighted she was about two to three miles away, and when she was about a half-mile of us she suddenly disappeared. There were four witnesses of this spectacle, the 2nd Officer, a Cadet, the helmsman and myself.

On December 5, 1872, the *Mary Celeste,* a Canadian-built 100-foot brigantine of 282 tons registered in New York, was found abandoned between Portugal and the nearby Azores. The ship was totally without crew but intact and under sail, heading toward the Strait of Gibraltar. The last log entry was eleven days prior to its discovery. The God-fearing, teetotal Captain Benjamin Spooner Briggs, his wife Sarah, two-year-old daughter Sophia Matilda, and the crew of seven were missing; nothing was to be seen or found of any of them ever again. The *Mary Celeste* is not, technically, a ghost ship but a mystery ship, or mystery story. However, it is usually listed as a ghost ship.

In 1933 a lifeboat was found floating in the area off the southwest coast of Vancouver Island. The boat was in very good condition, and yet it was from the wreck of the passenger steamship SS *Valencia,* which had sunk twenty-seven years before, in 1906. For many years after the *Valencia*'s sinking, sailors have reported seeing the ship itself in the area and reported that the apparition followed them along the coast.

In February 1948, a Morse code SOS message was picked up coming from the Dutch freighter *Ourang Medan*. Many ships responded to it. The *Ourang Medan* was found adrift off Indonesia with all of its crew—and the ship's dog—dead. The boarding party described the crew as being "frozen, teeth baring, gaping at the sun." Before the ship could be towed to a home port, it exploded and sank. The reason for the deaths is still unexplained. The origin and history of the ship is unknown.

In February 1748, the *Lady Lovibond*, a three-masted schooner, went down over the Goodwin Sands, a notoriously dangerous area off the coast of Kent, England. As many as 2,000 ships have been lost on this ten-mile stretch of sand banks. (In the great storm of 1703, thirteen men-of-war and forty merchant vessels were wrecked there, with the loss of 2,168 lives.) It's said that as many as 50,000 people altogether have lost their lives on these sand banks. The *Lady Lovibond* had been bound for Oporto, Portugal, carrying a cargo of flour, wine, meat, and gold. It's said that First Mate Rivers, jealous of Captain Simon Peel's marriage, deliberately ran the ship aground. All hands were lost. Subsequently, over the years, fishermen have reported seeing the craft. It is said that it reappears every fifty years on the anniversary of the disaster. The last sighting was in 1998.

Ghost Train

There is a short section of railroad track between the
North Street Bridge and the Junction in Pittsfield,
Massachusetts. It passes Union Depot. One day, in
early 1958, customers in the Bridge Lunch heard and
saw a train go by on this stretch of track. The train—an
old steam locomotive—has been described as consist-
ing of five or six coaches and a baggage car. No steam
trains had used that line for many years prior to the
sighting, yet a number of the diner's customers saw it
pass by. There was a repeat performance a month or so
later, when employees and customers again watched the
old train steam east toward Boston. Officials reported
no train activity—least of all steam train activity—on
that line at any time.

Ghost Vehicles

Phantom vehicles are often thought of in terms of
ancient coaches rushing along country roads on the
night of the full moon, but there are many examples of

modern phantom vehicles of the car, truck, and bus variety. Some of these are associated with vehicles that were involved in crashes and fatal accidents.

In the 1930s, there was a ghost bus seen on occasion in London. It was one of the old, red, double-decker buses, with the number 7, indicating that it traveled in the area of North Kensington. There was a very dangerous intersection—Saint Mark Boulevard and Cambridge Gardens—with blind corners; the site of many vehicle accidents. The acute angles of the roads were finally corrected, but before that was done several London Transport employees spoke of seeing the bus—"Old No. 7"—drive into the garage, sit for a few moments with its motor running, and then just disappear.

In that North Kensington area of London, on the night of June 15, 1934, a bus suddenly appeared driving straight for a young man in a car. The young man tried to avoid the bus, crashed into another car, and was killed. The bus—according to witnesses—was driverless and simply disappeared immediately after the accident. The same bus repeated its performance a number of times after that, over the years, though with none of the ensuing accidents being fatal. In the 1980s, a similar event happened when a man saw a phantom truck being driven straight at him. He had to swerve to avoid the truck, running into a light pole. The truck disappeared.

In Kent, England, on the Lamberhurst-Frant highway, there have been numerous reports of a truck suddenly appearing. It has caused drivers to swerve to avoid it, only for the drivers to see the truck fade to nothing. These appearances occur most often in the Christmas season.

At Borley Rectory, in the parish of Borley, Kent, in England—a place that was dubbed "the most haunted house in England" (though it has since been

demolished)—a large number of ghostly incidents were reported and investigated. One of the frequent reports was of the sound of a horse-drawn carriage driving up to the house. Nothing was ever seen, but the sound of this visitation was reported by various credible witnesses.

At a family farm in the Midwest, a phantom car, of mid-1930s vintage, was heard and on occasion seen coming up the driveway to the house and stopping. The car doors were heard to open and footsteps crunched on the gravel driveway, but then the car would vanish. This phantom visitor has appeared sporadically from the late 1930s to the present.

The *Silverpilen* subway train is supposed to haunt the metro system of Stockholm, the Swedish capital. The train has been dubbed "The Silver Arrow" because it is comprised of model C5 silver-colored cars dating from the 1960s (no longer used). A variety of urban legends have grown up around this train.

Literary Ghosts

Many are the ghosts that have become famous in literature. Charles Dickens's Victorian morality tale A Christmas Carol *has some of the best known, with the ghost of Jacob Marley leading Ebenezer Scrooge to the Ghosts of Christmas Past, Christmas Present, and Christmas Yet to Come. This journey has a profound effect on Scrooge and turns him from a cheerless, uncaring skinflint into a loving, generous, kind-hearted soul.*

In Shakespeare's Hamlet, *the ghost of the young prince's father, King Hamlet, appears four times, and each time terrorizes those to whom he appears. He appears in order to tell his son, the prince, the manner of his death and to ask Hamlet to avenge him. The character of the king is loosely based on Horwendill, a legendary Jutish chieftain mentioned in Saxo Grammaticus's* Gesta Danorum *and in the* Chronicon Lethrense.

Oscar Wilde's novella The Canterbury Ghost *has all the ingredients of a "traditional" ghost story, with clanking chains and creaking floorboards set in an ancient English manor house. The work is a comedy and has been retold and reworked over the years, as a book, play, several films, an opera, radio play, and the theme of more than one popular song. It is very much a parody of the traditional ghost story.*

Blithe Spirit *is Noel Coward's comedic play about a man haunted by the ghost of his first wife, who appears after the husband's attendance at a Spiritualist séance. The ghost tries to antagonize the second wife and upset the marriage. Twenty-six years after it was written, a version of it was presented as a Broadway musical directed by Noel Coward. There have been stage, film, and television versions of it. In recent years there have been films that followed the same theme, and variations on it* (Over Her Dead Body, *for example*).

The Turn of the Screw *is a short ghost story by Henry James, first published in 1898. It has been said that James relates the amount of light present in various scenes to the strength of the supernatural or ghostly forces apparently at work. He employs the traditional old building settings but leaves it to the reader to decide whether or not the figures seen by the narrating governess are actually ghosts or simply figments of her imagination.*

The Legend of Sleepy Hollow, *by Washington Irving, must rank high on the popularity scale of ghost stories. There have been a number of movies based on* the story. Interestingly, the ghost in the story—that of a Headless Hessian horseman—is almost certainly not a ghost at all, but the very real (in the story) Abraham "Brom Bones" Van Brunt, the town rowdy who competes with Ichabod Crane for the hand of Katrina Van Tassel, the daughter of a wealthy farmer. The overall theme of a wild ghostly chase follows the tradition of such old folktales as Robert Burns's "Tam O'Shanter," written in 1790.

There are hundreds of ghost stories in literature: American ghost stories, English ghost stories, Victorian ghost stories, and so on. Many have been adapted for the big and small screen: Ghost; Over Her Dead Body; The Ghost and Mrs. Muir; Wuthering Heights; Portrait of Jennie; Letter from an Unknown Woman; The Uninvited; Liliom; Truly, Madly, Deeply; Michael; City of Angels, for example.

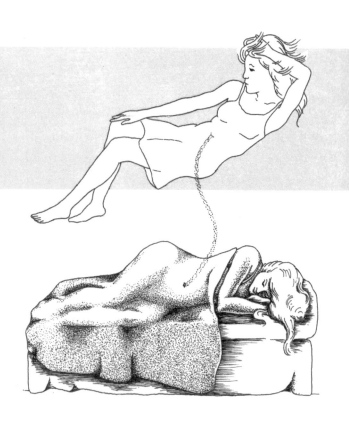

Living Ghosts

*Ghosts of the living are more properly apparitions (from the Latin apparere, "to appear"). Such a ghost is most likely to appear when the living person is asleep, in a trance, in meditation, or even just lost in a daydream. The astral body (see **Astral Bodies**) of the person separates from the physical body and travels about. Its journeys may be observed by those with psychic abilities, or may even appear to the person they are "visiting" whose psychic abilities are not normally fully tuned.*

Astral Bodies

The ancient Egyptians, the early Greeks, the Hebrews, and many more believed that the human body had an invisible double (the *ka*; *eidolon*; *ruach*) that could, in sleep, separate from its physical counterpart and travel the world at will. This is more commonly known as the astral body, or "etheric double." It is connected to the physical by an invisible and infinitely elastic silver cord. At death this cord separates but otherwise remains connected no matter where the astral body should travel. Some sensitives can see a thin dark outline around any living body and recognize that as the astral double. It is believed that dreams are in fact the remembered fragments of your astral journeys while asleep.

There have been many examples of someone seeing a ghost and believing it indicated the death of the person they were seeing, only to find that in fact that person was still very much alive. When comparing times of the sighting, it is usually found that the person appearing in ghostly form was, in fact, either asleep at that time or in some trancelike state.

Zombies

The zombie of Vodoun is a living corpse, a human ghost. It is a person who has apparently died and then been brought back to life. There have been documented cases of Haitians who have had a family member die unexpectedly and have buried him or her only to hear that someone has seen the "deceased" many months or even years later. The "ghost" is usually mute and in a greatly debilitated state, barely skin and bone and dressed in rags. The word *zombie* comes from the Congolese *nvumbi* meaning "a person deprived of its soul."

In Haiti, where most zombies are found, the dead are not embalmed but put into a wooden coffin and buried as quickly a possible. A *boko* is a magician or sorcerer who deals in magic and charms. Most bokos are unscrupulous and will place a curse on anyone for a fee. (They will then remove that curse if the person affected pays a higher fee.) It is the bokos who are responsible for zombies, creating them as a means of cheap labor.

An alkaloid drug is introduced into the victim. This is a drug that produces a cataleptic state easily mistaken for death. Often there is no death certificate asked for or issued and, with the heat and humidity, the body is put into the ground as quickly as possible. By the night-time the main effects of the drug have worn off, and the boko can dig up the "corpse" and administer an anti-dote, then lead away the victim into a life of servitude.

What drugs would be used for this? The most obvious would be *Atropa belladonna, Hyoscyamus niger,* and various species of *Datura.* There are other locally available narcotics such as *Terminalia catappa,* *Hippomane mancinella,* and *Spondias dulcis;* all deadly poisons if used incautiously.

Materializations

*Materialization, taking place at a Spiritualist séance,
is a collaboration of spirit and medium. The physical
body of the medium exudes a substance called ectoplasm.
Spirit takes the ectoplasm and "clothes" itself so the form
of the spirit becomes apparent to the sitters . . . the spirit
materializes.*

Ectoplasm

The Greek words *ekto* and *plasma*, meaning "exteriorized substance" give us the modern word *ectoplasm*. This word was coined by Professor Charles Richet in 1894 and applied to a materialized spirit or ghost, as seen at a Spiritualist séance. When a "physical" (as opposed to a "mental") medium goes into trance, he or she may exude a white substance known as ectoplasm. This streams from the body out of a variety of orifices, such as the nose, ears, mouth, navel, nipples, sexual organs, or even just from the pores. Apparently it is light sensitive, requiring complete darkness to manifest. In the early days of Spiritualism, this fact led to many fraudulent mediums producing ersatz ectoplasm in the form of cheesecloth, gauze, and the like, smuggled into the séance room and produced at the appropriate moment. This fraudulent practice was ended with the advent of infrared photography, though not before many fake mediums were unmasked. Yet this same infrared photography was the means of proving the existence of actual ectoplasm, as revealed in photographs of the British medium Jack Weber, for example.

Extrusions of ectoplasm might be used to move objects, such as trumpets (aluminum megaphones used to amplify spirit voices), tables, chairs, or even people. However, the most remarkable appearance of ectoplasm was when it manifested alongside the medium and formed into the shape of the departed spirit being contacted. Sitters at a séance could recognize the deceased loved one. This materialization would sometimes move and even speak. On occasion it could be touched, though if done so without the spirit's permission the ectoplasm immediately retracted into the medium's body.

Materializations also occur outside the séance room. In the Bible (Matthew 17) two long-deceased men, Elijah and Moses, materialize in solid form to Jesus and three apostles. Historical ghosts (*vide*) and many others have materialized, either in transparent form or in solid form, and have been photographed with and without infrared.

Monsters

The definition of monster is "a frightening legendary figure" with the emphasis on "frightening." Monsters are usually of hideous appearance and may be malformed humans or animals or pure otherworldly demons. They feature in folktales and fairy tales and in the myths and legends of many countries.

Agaberte

In Scandinavian legend, Agaberte is the daughter of the giant Vagnoste. She can appear in almost any shape. She usually disguised herself as a fragile old woman, ancient and wrinkled, much like the Scottish

Cailleach Bheur. However, in an instant Agaberte could transform herself from very weak to extremely strong, changing into a giantess whose head reached to the clouds. People believed her to be capable of nearly anything.

Anneberg

Anneberg is a spirit or ghost that appears to miners in Germany. He frequently appears in the form of a demon with a horse's head. His breath has been said to have killed a dozen miners in a silver mine.

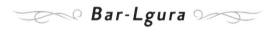

Babau

A French spirit said to devour children. Its legend dates back to the twelfth century when it was depicted as a dragonlike creature. At that time it had breached the walls of the town of Rivesaltes and ate a number of children. One of the monster's bones is today on display in the Tourist Information Office of Rivesaltes, a town in the Pyrénées-Orientales département in southwestern France.

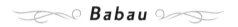

Bar-Lgura

An ancient Semitic entity that sits on the roofs of houses and leaps on the inhabitants when they show themselves. Those so attacked are referred to as *d'baregara*.

Ch'iang Shich

A Chinese monster spirit or ghost that takes over the body of an unburied corpse. It revives the corpse, bringing it to a semblance of life, and then wreaks death and destruction.

Rakshasa

A frightening but dim-witted Indian spirit that can take many forms, including those of animals and birds. Its favorite guise, however, is as a beautiful woman. The name *rakshasa* means "destroyer" and it lives up to its name. Anyone touched by a rakshasa will die. Like the Chinese *ch'iang shich*, it can reanimate a dead body, though is more likely to eat the corpse.

 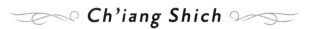

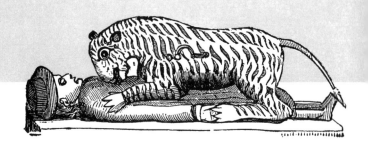

Mythical Ghosts;
Folklore Ghosts

*The myths and folklore of virtually all peoples include sto-
ries of ghosts. Christian mythology, as found in the Bible,
is a good example (see **Biblical Ghosts**). Many such
stories deal with benevolent ghosts; others are decidedly
malevolent. There are far too many such tales to include
them all, but here are some representative stories.*

 Afrit

In Arabian mythology, an *afrit* is the ghost of a murdered man who is intent on avenging his death. The
ghost leaves the body at the moment of death and
can be seen, by the sensitive, rising up in the form of

a vapor. If a new nail is driven into the blood-stained ground at that time, then the formation of the afrit can be avoided.

Ankou

The *ankou* is the King of the Dead in Brittany. There are ankous in every parish, since the last person to die during a year takes that position and holds it till the following year. The ankou (always a male) is described as tall and thin, wearing a wide-brimmed hat. He is accompanied by a rickety old cart, pulled by either two or four horses (varies in different districts), into which he puts the souls of the dead. One legend is that the original Ankou was the first child of Adam and Eve.

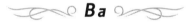

Ba

The *ba* is a version of the ancient Egyptian *ka* (*see page 21*). It remains with a dead body, in the tomb, only leaving at night to roam the vicinity.

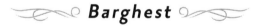

Barghest

Mostly found in the southwest of England—Somerset, Devon, and Cornwall—the *barghest* is a spectral hound that appears as an omen of death. It is also found in the north of England, in Lancashire and Yorkshire, where it is sometimes referred to as "The Shrieker" or "Shriker" because of the frightening sounds it makes when invisible.

Blue-cap

Similar in some ways to Germany's Anneberg, though more benevolent, the Blue-cap, or Blue-bonnet, is found in British coal mines. It is said to assist the miners in their search for veins, yet it has to be paid for its aid. Guiley[3] says, "Blue-cap's wages were left in a corner of the mine every two weeks. If they were below what he felt he deserved, the spirit indignantly rejected the sum. If the wages were above what he felt he earned, he left the excess amount."

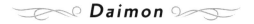

Daimon

The Greek *daimon*, or *dæmon*, could be either good or evil. They were quite distinct from the Christian "demons," being "supernatural beings between mortals and gods, such as inferior divinities and ghosts of dead heroes" (see Plato's *Symposium*). They were generally considered to be the guardians of mortals. The daimon of a dead hero could give protection and bring good fortune to those who showed respect.

[3] *The Encyclopedia of Ghosts and Spirits*: New York; Facts on File, 1992.

Nature Ghosts

Nature spirits are generally benevolent, though they can be easily upset. Their primary concern is with nature—plants, trees, animals, and so on. They will brook no interference with the natural ways. Carl Jung said that nature spirits were an early stage of human evolution. Probably because of the advancing development found in so many areas destroying natural acreage, few nature spirits show themselves to humans. However, on occasion they will do so, appearing in any one of many forms, often as a ghostly apparition.

Nature spirits are often referred to as devas. The word is from the Sanskrit, meaning "a being of brilliant light." One of the best recorded instances of working with nature spirits was the Findhorn project led by Peter

Caddy in the 1960s. The area Caddy started with was a barren, windswept section on the coast of Inverness, Scotland. It was a truly inhospitable place with sandy soil and sparse, desertlike life. With his wife Eileen and some friends, Caddy invoked the help of the local nature spirits to the point where the now fertile section produces such amazing harvests as 42-pound cabbages and 60-pound broccoli plants! There are sixty-five different vegetables now grown there, with twenty-one types of fruit, forty-two herbs, and beautiful flowers. But everything produced there is acknowledged to have come with the help of the nature spirits. While developing the area, many of the workers claimed to have seen them.

Akathaso

In Burma the *akathaso* are nature spirits that inhabit trees. Unlike most nature spirits, however, the akathaso are considered evil. They will harm anyone who tries to cut down a tree, or even to trim its limbs.

Tree Ghosts

There are many stories of tree spirits to be found in Native American folklore and in the folklore and mythology of many if not most peoples. In Norse mythology is found Yggdrasil, the World Tree. It is a great ash tree located at the center of the universe, and it joins the nine worlds of Norse cosmology. In India most

shrines are built underneath trees, with the belief that the vegetation is home to benevolent spirits. In Greek mythology tree spirits are called *Dryads*. Originally they were especially connected to oak trees (the Greek *drys* means "oak"), though the term came to be applied to all tree nymphs in general.

It is not unusual for people to catch glimpses of tree ghosts or spirits when passing through ancient woods. Lumberjacks have reported glimpses of angry tree spirits, and there have even been "accidents" to such workers that they have ascribed to these spirits.

Omen Ghosts;
Prophetic Ghosts

*There are both personal and general omens: those that
pertain to individuals and those that are generally
recognized and accepted. The Romans placed faith in
omens, seeking them out through augury. However, most
omens are based on the appearance or actions of a specific
person, animal, or bird. Omen ghosts, on the other hand,*

tend to appear suddenly and without warning; without being sought out.

One of the most common examples of an omen—usually for bad luck—is that of a cat crossing the path. But to see an apparition of a black cat crossing one's path is far more potent! Omen ghosts appear, deliver their message (in effect), and then disappear.

Banshee

One of the best known Irish ghosts is the banshee (*bean sídhe*), a harbinger of death. The name means "woman of the mounds" or "female fairy." Sir Walter Scott said, "The distinction of a Banshee is only allowed to families of the pure Milesian stock, and is never ascribed to any descendent of the proudest Norman or the boldest Saxon who followed the banner of Strongbow, much less to adventurers of later dates who have obtained settlements in the Green Isle." He would have one believe, therefore, that only the purest, oldest, and highest born of the Irish are ever visited by a banshee. Certainly the O'Rourkes, O'Brians, O'Malleys, and the O'Donnals—all great families—have been visited by the banshee over several generations.

It has been said that a banshee is really the disembodied soul of someone who once lived and was attached to the family in some way. It depends upon the relationship that the banshee had with the dying family member as to how the banshee announces his or her coming death. If the person about to die was of a gentle, kind disposition, then the banshee will appear and sing soft songs of warning, summoning the person to death. But if the person destined to die was of a hateful disposition, then the banshee will make her announcement with horrible cries and screams.

There have been many instances of a banshee being seen. She has been described as sometimes young and beautiful but sometimes old and haggard. She wears a red or green dress covered by a gray, hooded cloak. She becomes visible at night, approaches a house, and starts out with a mournful keening wail said by some to sound like the moaning of the wind. If you hear the cry of the banshee, it means there will be a death in the family; if you see the banshee, then it is you who will die.

The people of Wales have their own version of the banshee, known to them as the *gwrach-y-rhibyn*, meaning "Old Hag of the Dribble."

Bean-Nighe

The *bean-nighe* is the Scottish version of the banshee. The word is Scottish Gaelic for "washer woman," since she is often seen at deserted streams washing blood from the grave clothes of those about to die. It is said that a bean-nighe is a woman who died in childbirth and who is now doomed to warn others of approaching death. In the ancient Celtic epic, *The Ulster Cycle*, the Morrígan is seen in the role of a bean-nighe.

Black Shuck

In British folklore, the Black Shuck is a large black dog that appears prior to someone's death. To meet Black Shuck is a sure sign that you will die within a year. On dark nights its demonic howl can be heard, most especially in areas of East Anglia and in the southwest of England. The dog haunts graveyards, marshes, and lonely country roads. It is said to be the size of a young calf and has eyes that glow bright red or yellow (some say green).

Other names that have been applied to Black Shuck include Galleytrot, Ol' Doofus, Shug Monkey, Churchyard Beast, Hellbeast, and Swooning Shadow. Many folktales of impending death include a big black ghost dog, often associated with the devil.

Doppelgänger

A *doppelgänger* (German for "double walker" or "double goer") is the apparition of the double of a living person—a complete duplicate in every way. Also known as a *fetch*, it usually appears only moments before the person's death and seems to be solid, though there have been reports of some doppelgängers that it was possible to see through. The poet Percy Shelley saw his doppelgänger moments before he drowned. In Carl Sandburg's biography of Abraham Lincoln, Sandburg says, "On the evening of (Lincoln's) election he had thrown himself on one of the haircloth sofas at home, just after the first telegrams of November 6 had told him he was elected President, and looking into a bureau mirror across the room he saw himself full length, but with two faces. It bothered him; he got up; the illusion vanished; but when he lay down again there in the glass again were two faces, one paler than the other."

Today, *doppelgänger* is used to refer to any look-alike person, whether or not they may be a harbinger of death, though they are still thought to indicate coming bad luck.

Drummer of Cortachy

In medieval times, a messenger from a feuding clan brought bad news to Ogilvy, Earl of Airlie, at Cortachy Castle in Angus, Scotland. In a rage, Ogilvy stuffed the messenger into his own drum and had him hurled from the castle battlements. The drummer survived the fall long enough to curse the Ogilvy family, saying that he would return and beat his drum to signal an impending family death. This has been the case up until as recently as 1900 when the then Earl died in the Boer War. Since that time the drum has been silent.

There are many recorded accounts of the drum being heard, by guests and by family members. In 1844 a Miss Dalrymple was staying at the castle and heard the drumming. Lady Airlie subsequently died. Just five years later, an Englishman guest heard the drumming; the ninth Earl of Airlie died the following day.

Ekimmu

Ekimmu means "that which is snatched away." It was a ghost that might attach itself to anyone. It was found in ancient Assyria and was believed to be the ghost of someone who suffered a violent death such as murder, death in battle, drowning, and so on. When found wailing outside a house, it indicated that someone in the house was about to die.

Fetch

A fetch is much like a doppelgänger (*see page 114*) or a wraith. It is the double of someone who is about to die, though in Ireland, if seen in the early morning, it can presage a long life. The fetch is found in English and Irish folklore. Fetches can be seen by anyone but are mostly seen by those with psychic abilities. The death that signals the appearance of the fetch may be immediate or it may be weeks or even months in coming.

Herne the Hunter

Herne the Hunter, sometimes spectral leader of the Wild Hunt, is most often seen as the forecaster of catastrophe on a national level. He is seen riding with his hounds in the Great Park of Windsor Castle, in England. He rides a black horse and is most generally seen with stag's antlers growing from his head. Herne is associated with the ancient pagan hunting god and is said to ride out when England is in danger. There were many reports of him being sighted prior to World Wars I and II.

Kelpie

A Scottish water spirit. It is said that if you see a Kelpie then you will die, probably from drowning. Kelpies usually appear in the shape of a gray horse on the banks of a lake or river. They will be grazing peacefully, tempting the observer to ride them. But once mounted, the Kelpie will rush off into the water, drowning the rider and then eating him. To see a Kelpie is a sure sign of coming death.

Seven Whistlers

The Seven Whistlers are Lancashire wild geese. When seven of them fly over at night, their cries can be taken as an omen of coming death. Nineteenth-century coal miners and seamen very much believed in them, since both groups thought whistling to be unlucky. If a miner heard the cries, he had to immediately stop work and go home, or disaster would find him. In Leicestershire it was believed that the seven were the ghosts of colliers who had died in the mines. In neighboring Lancashire it was said that the colliers had whistled despite the superstition against it and had subsequently been carried away by a whirlwind.

Vardøgr

Meaning "forerunner," a *Vardøgr* is a little like a doppelgänger in that it is a double of a person. But this double appears in advance of the actual person, to announce his or her arrival. Others may see the Vardøgr and speak to it, believing it to be the actual person. They are then surprised when the person arrives some time later, dressed exactly as was seen.

Poltergeists

The word poltergeist is from the German and means "noisy ghost," but in fact a poltergeist is not a ghost. It is raw energy, albeit of a psychic type. It has been defined as "recurrent spontaneous psychokinesis." Psychokinesis is the movement of objects without physical contact with them.

A ghost is the spirit, materialization, or appearance of a deceased person or animal. A poltergeist has no connection with the deceased. It has been found that most poltergeist activity takes place when there is a child or young person around the age of puberty in the vicinity. There seems to be some connection with the energy

*produced and given off by the child at that time. This
energy causes objects to fly through the air of their own
volition. Plates and cups may smash against walls, tables
and chairs be tossed about, doors slam, lights flash on and
off. Not all poltergeist activity is centered around a child,
however. A person of any age who is going through some
sort of emotional crisis can produce the same results.*

Amityville "Horror"

Located at 112 Ocean Avenue, Amityville, Long
Island, New York, the home of George and Kathy Lutz
became infamous, in 1975, as a center for poltergeist
activity. The Lutzes claimed that one of the causes for
the disturbances was the fact that a little over a year
before, the previous occupants of the house, Ronald
and Louise DeFeo and four of their children, had been
murdered by the oldest child, Ronald Jr.

Although many psychics who initially investigated the house (including this author, members of
the Psychical Research Foundation, and the American
Society for Psychical Research) could find no indication of psychic activity, let alone negative or poltergeist
activity, the Lutzes persisted in their claims of paranormal phenomena. Some years later it was revealed that
they and their lawyer William Weber concocted the
whole story while sitting around the kitchen table shar-
ing a bottle of wine. Interestingly, the events that were

supposed to have happened to the Lutzes came on the heels of the movie *The Exorcist* (1973). It might also be noted that subsequent owners of the house (Jim and Barbara Cromarty were the immediate next owners) have not reported any unusual activity there at all. The first major book on the event was written by Jay Anson, who never actually visited the house.

One of the explanations offered by a notable ghost hunter was that the house had been built (in 1928) on the site of a Native American burial ground. Native American and other historians have proven this to be completely untrue.

 Boggart

The boggart is an exception to the rule in that it is a spirit—a form of hobgoblin—that causes poltergeist-like activity to take place. It can be simply mischievous or it can be downright vindictive. Boggart activity is usually accompanied by laughter or terrible screeching, which helps separate it from pure poltergeist activity. Boggarts are found in British folklore, being prominent in Lancashire, Yorkshire, and the industrial north as a whole. It is said that they can inhabit the body of an animal (*see* **Dybbuk**, *page 127*).

Cock Lane Ghost

The notorious Cock Lane Ghost—of Smithfield, London, England—caused quite a commotion from 1762 to 1764. It seemed that poltergeist activity was taking place around Elizabeth, the twelve-year-old daughter of the house's owner, a Mr. Parsons, who was a parish clerk in the nearby church. But there was more than just the regular poltergeist activity; there were spirit rappings that seemed to indicate that the current tenant of the house, a Mr. Kent, had murdered his sister-in-law. A committee was set up to investigate. This was led by Dr. Samuel Johnson and the Rev. Mr. Douglas (later Bishop of Salisbury). Although Parsons reported much activity, it was found that nothing would happen in the presence of the committee. Suspicions were aroused, and it was eventually determined that Parsons had concocted the whole thing because he had borrowed money from Kent and couldn't repay it. Kent's sister-in-law had, in fact, died of smallpox. Parsons went to trial, was found guilty, and spent time in the pillory before being imprisoned.

Dodleston Poltergeist

The poltergeist haunting of a small house in Dodleston, Chester, England, began with a message appearing on a computer. It was in 1984—before home computers were common and well before e-mail—and the message came through on a computer that Ken, a teacher, had borrowed from school. At first he thought it was a joke, but then a message appeared that said:

> I write on behalf of many. What strange words you speak, although, I must confess that I too have been badly educated. Sometimes it seems that changes are obstructive, for many a time they disturb me sleeping in my bed. You are a worthy man who has a fanciful woman and you live in my house. I have no wish to alarm you, for it is only since the half-witted fool ripped apart my confines have I been tormented at nights. I have seen many changes (lastly the schoolhouse and your home). It is a fitting place, with lights which the devil makes, and costly things, which only my friend Edmund Grey can afford, or the king himself. It was a great crime to have stolen my house. LW

The sender of the message, who later gave his name as "Lukas," sent many more messages over the next few months. Ken and Debbie, the homeowners, learned that his real name was Tomas Harden and that he was unhappy with the renovation work they were doing in the house. There were considerable poltergeist phenomena, with chairs being thrown about and pet food containers being emptied; there was a lot of destruction. Sometimes Lukas's messages would be written on the stone floor, in chalk, in an elaborate hand. Over a two-year period about 300 messages were received, via the computer and on the floor, before the spirit went away and the disruption ended.

The Weiser Field Guide to Ghosts

Drummer of Tedworth

This story was first given in Joseph Glanville's *Saducismus Triumphatus* in 1668. It's the true tale of a phantom drummer that manifested in the home of magistrate John Mompesson in April 1661. In the little town of Tedworth, in Wiltshire, England, an itinerant magician and drummer named William Drury was caught in shady dealings. He was charged, found guilty, and his drum was confiscated. He was made to leave the district, and his drum was placed in the home of the magistrate John Mompesson.

Mompesson had to travel away from home for a few days and returned to be told many stories of strange disturbances and noises coming from his empty house, especially at night. There was banging on the roof, rappings on walls, and always the beating of a drum. The drum played roundheads, cuckolds, and tattoos at all hours of the day and night. Mompesson immediately had Drury's drum destroyed, broken into pieces. But the sounds continued.

The Reverend Joseph Glanville was chaplain to King Charles II. He went to investigate. At the house he found two young girls, aged seven and eleven, sitting up in bed and very frightened. There was scratching coming from the walls, ceiling, and even the bedhead, yet Glanville could readily see the girls' hands at all times. Other strange things happened, none explainable.

Mompesson learned that the drummer Drury had been arrested for theft in the neighboring town of Gloucester. He was transported out of the country to the colonies, and the sounds finally ceased. But some time later they started up again. It transpired that Drury had managed to work his way back to England. The drumming in Mompesson's house became worse than ever. In addition there was other poltergeist activity—windows shook, chamberpots were emptied onto the floor, beds were shaken, sulfurous smells permeated the house. Some of the noises were so loud that they could be heard in the rest of the village. Then suddenly, for no apparent reason, everything stopped. There were no further disturbances, no further banging of the drum. What had become of Drury was unknown, but it seems likely that he had met his death, bringing the poltergeist activity to an end.

Possessive Ghosts

There are a few ghosts that will take possession of living beings. The dybbuk is one of these; the boggart is another, though the latter usually restricts its activities to possessing animals and birds. The possessed person or animal will then have no control over its own thoughts and actions, being completely controlled by the possessing spirit.

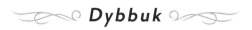

Dybbuk

Various ghosts can take possession of the living, if only for a short period. The boggart (*see page 121*), for example, can possess a dog or a cat. But a *dybbuk*, in

Jewish folklore, will take possession of humans, speaking through their mouth and manipulating their body. In earlier times these evil spirits were termed *ibbur* (spirits), but *dybbuk* was the term used by German and Polish Jews and became the more common word.

There are various methods for exorcizing a dybbuk, or dybbukim (plural), given in the Qabbalah, though the exorcism must be performed by a "miracle-working" rabbi. A dybbuk does not know that he or she is dead.

Religious Ghosts

*Apparitions of religious figures—both deities and
priests—have appeared to many people over the years.
A prime example is the figure of the Virgin Mary, which
has been seen in locations around the world. Many times
a figure is presumed to be a particular religious figure
when in fact it could be another. For example, some of
the appearances attributed to Mary, the mother of Jesus,
could as well be one of the many forms of the Mother
Goddess as acknowledged by Neopagans and Wiccans.
The Bible is replete with stories of the ghost of Jesus appearing to his disciples.*

 Jesus

Appearances of Jesus are recorded in the Bible, but
there have been modern-day sightings of him also.

Many of these have been to soldiers in peril on the battlefield (Edouard-Bernard Debat-Ponsan's painting of Jesus appearing to soldiers is a beautiful rendition of such an example). The apparition of Jesus has appeared to people in automobile accidents and train wrecks in a wide variety of circumstances.

Mary

By far the majority of religious apparitions seem to have been of Mary, mother of Jesus. But here again many such appearances may well be of figures other than Mary: Gaia, Isis, Bride, Devi, Kali, Erzuli, and so on. In fact, the Roman Catholic Church has acknowledged only seven appearances as being of Mary: Guadalupe, Mexico (1531); Paris, France (1830); La

Salette, France (1846); Lourdes, France (1858); Fatima, Portugal (1917); Beauraing, Belgium (1932); and Banneaux, Belgium (1933). Interestingly, all but two have been in France or its neighbor Belgium.

Yet as with the believed appearances of Jesus, there have been innumerable appearances of Mary and goddess figures to individuals in times of crisis and need. It would seem that any deeply religious person—regardless of the particular religion—may encounter what amounts to a ghost of their personal deity.

 Pele

Pele—or "Madame Pele"—is Hawaii's goddess of fire, lightning, dance, volcanoes, and violence. There are various myths about her origins, but she is mainly associated with Hawaii's volcanoes, particularly on the eastern side of Mauna Loa.

Pele is very beautiful "with a back straight as a cliff and breasts rounded like the moon." She has many lovers. Her apparition appears as a young and beautiful woman, frequently dressed in a bright red muumuu and most often seen in the early morning hours, walking along a deserted road. You should stop to offer her a lift, otherwise she will become extremely angry, and her wrath is something to be avoided at all costs!

Photographs of fiery eruptions have included what looked like the face of Pele. She is well respected by Christians, Buddhists, Shinto, and others. Since 1983 she has destroyed more than a hundred structures on the Big Island and has added more than seventy acres of land to the island's southeastern coastline.

Pele has been encountered by drivers who think they are picking up an old woman dressed all in white, usually accompanied by a little dog, on roads in Kilauea National Park. But then they look in the rearview mirror to find that the backseat is empty.

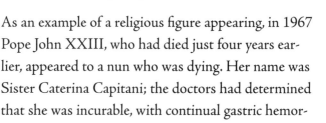

Pope John XXIII

As an example of a religious figure appearing, in 1967 Pope John XXIII, who had died just four years earlier, appeared to a nun who was dying. Her name was Sister Caterina Capitani; the doctors had determined that she was incurable, with continual gastric hemorrhages following surgery. As she lay in a hospital bed in Naples, Italy, she suddenly felt a soothing hand on her abdomen and was surprised to see the deceased pope standing by her bed. Although he was not in his papal regalia, she recognized him. He proclaimed, "You are healed!" and told her to call her doctors and the other sisters, which she did. They found her fully recovered.

Shadow Ghosts

Most ghosts caught on film, if not appearing as normal people, have a whitish mistiness about them. Many times, in fact, there is nothing caught but the white mist. So-called shadow ghosts are just the opposite: they are dark, frequently black, vaguely human figures. They may be caught on film but are more often sighted in peripheral vision, out of the corner of your eye. They have been broken down into three main categories: Type A (appearing as a dark misty shape hovering above the ground), Type B (large, dense, dark cloud ranging from 2 to 8 feet in height), and Type C (appearing in human form, sometimes wearing a hat, but as much as 8 feet in height).

Shadow ghosts are known in folklore (modern and traditional) and are also found in Native American traditional beliefs. Reports of sightings seldom if ever include descriptions of facial features, clothing type, or other details, because the apparitions are so vague and tenuous, akin to silhouettes. Witnesses also state that there is not the same "feeling" experienced as when a more normal ghost is encountered. There is more a sense of fear and dread. And yet there is no indication of evil associated with shadow ghosts. It is probably the inbred unconscious association that we make between dark or black and negativity or evil.

Energy Lines

Sometimes a photograph will not show a ghost in the sense of a human or animal figure or even a white mist. On occasion there is a bright, sharply defined, white or colored line of energy on the picture. It might look like a miniature bolt of lightning. This is caused by a ghost or spirit trying to manifest. It indicates that there is energy building but not yet formed into any coherent shape.

Spirits

The majority of ghosts are the spirits or souls of the deceased who once lived on the earth plane. Here the term "Spirit" is also used to apply to those entities which are inhuman and have had no such earthly existence. Such spirits were conjured by ceremonial magicians, in the Middle Ages, it being believed that to show control over such a creature was to open the door to all manner of powers that the spirits possessed. Many of these spirits would appear in grotesque form (see also **Monsters**).

Agathion

A familiar spirit that only shows itself at midday. It can appear as a human or an animal and can enclose itself in a bottle, a talisman, or a magic ring. It is a benevolent spirit, a protective entity.

Bogey

A hobgoblin; a friendly spirit with a great sense of humor. The name comes from the Scandinavian *bog*, meaning "god." Variations are *boggart*, *bogle*, *bug-a-boo*, *barquest*, *boquest*, *boman*, *bol*, and *bock*.

Bommasso

Of Indian origin, the *Bommasso* is found in Burma. It is one of the *nats*, or spirits, that are found throughout every home. They hide in the corners of rooms and in closets. The Bommasso can be spirits of the dead and are then greatly feared by the Burmese people. When there is a death, the body must be got into the ground immediately, taking the very shortest possible route to the graveyard.

Bucca; bocca

This spirit often appears in the form of a goat and was originally a fertility deity native to Cornwall, England.

Fishermen left it offerings of fish on the beach. It was later "downgraded" to a sprite, much like Puck. There are children's tales of *buccas* working in tin mines in Cornwall. These spirits will grant wishes in exchange for food. In Cornwall, a storm blowing from a south-westerly direction was referred to as "bucca calling."

Diakka

Andrew Jackson Davis—known as the Poughkeepsie Seer—used the term *Diakka* to describe those spirits that were ignorant and undeveloped. There is an old metaphysical saying: "Like attracts like." This is seen in the fact that unscrupulous people presenting themselves as mediums attract Diakka to themselves and then produce fraudulent séances employing trickery to deceive the sitters.

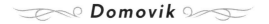

Domovik

A Russian household spirit. There is one found in every home. When seen, the *Domovik* appears as an old man with gray or white hair and a beard. It is believed that he was the original patriarch of the family.

The Domovik lives behind the stove, from where he watches over everyone in the household, assisting in family chores. It is believed that if the family members upset the Domovik, he will bring about poltergeist-like phenomena and even—as an extreme—burn down the house.

Ekimmu

In ancient Assyria, the *Ekimmu* was the spirit of someone who died an untimely death, by murder, suicide, in battle, drowning, or similar (*see also* **Omen Ghosts**). It was very much a nuisance because it could attach itself to anyone and haunt them. If improper graveside rites were administered, then an Ekimmu could result. If a person died without leaving kin, then an Ekimmu would search out someone to whom it could attach itself.

Ghoul

Ghouls are believed to inhabit graveyards, though they may also be found at any old ruins. In Islamic lore, they feed on the flesh of humans, especially children. They steal fresh corpses from graves. In India the ghoul is known as a *Vetala*. Ghouls are only seen at night and, like zombies, look like emaciated humans.

Goblin

Generally of a mischievous nature, these spirits are found in homes. They are frequently of grotesque appearance and can be very unpredictable. They can, if in a good mood, help the inhabitants of the home with small tasks but are just as likely to play tricks. It's said that they are especially attracted to homes with children, and children are more likely to actually see these spirits. They are common in many parts of Great Britain but may be found in other parts of the world. In Germany they are called *Kobolds*. They are allied with bogeys. They can produce poltergeist-type phenomena if provoked.

Gremlin

Gremlins came into being during World War I but came to prominence during the World War II. They are associated with airplanes, especially fighters, and are the spirits that cause things to go wrong. Guns jamming, engine problems, landing gear hangups: all were the work of gremlins, the pilots and ground crew believed. The spirits would block pipes and open valves, loosen screws, and break rivets. It has been suggested that the name comes from the Old English *gremian*, meaning "to vex."

Gremlins have been seen by pilots and aircrew in flight, often as vague, goblinlike creatures hanging onto wings and other parts of the airplane, though their exact description varies. They can be friendly and have also been credited with helping pilots safely bring home battle-torn aircraft. In his book *The Spirit of St. Louis* (1953), Charles Lindberg speaks of apparitions that appeared to him when he became extremely fatigued flying solo across the Atlantic. They advised him on navigation and encouraged him on the flight, acting exactly as many reported incidents of gremlins during the war.

In recent times, two workmen were preparing a display at the Tangmere Museum in England. (Tangmere was one of the busy fighter stations in the early days of World War II.) They were working late and the only ones in the building. Hearing noises, they moved down a hall to investigate, thinking someone might have broken in. Suddenly a 3-foot length of 2x4 wood came bouncing along the ground toward them, like a Pogo stick but with no one on it! One of the workmen shouted, "All right! That's enough!" The piece of wood stopped, stood for a moment, and then fell over. The workmen returned to what they had been doing only to find that the hammer belonging to one of them had disappeared. As they looked around, the hammer suddenly appeared on a table some distance away. Again one of them shouted, "All right! You win!" They firmly believe that it was gremlins making their presence known. Similar stories have been told by others who have been at Tangmere either in the museum or during the construction of the museum. There was another instance of a Pogo stick length of wood and also of a disappearing pencil that suddenly reappeared when its owner pleaded for the gremlins to stop fooling about.

Gunna

A Scottish spirit of the Highlands. They always are alone—it has been suggested that the *Gunna* has been banished from fairyland—and are difficult to see. The

Gunna wears foxskins and brown or green leather. He has a love of cattle and will sometimes look after cattle when the herdsman has been drawn away.

Ifrits

Of Arabian origin, *Ifrits* feature in Persian and Indian mythology and folklore. They are hideous-looking creatures that inhabit wild places, including woods, cemeteries, and ruined buildings. They can change their shape and appear in many guises. They will attack any living creature.

Incubus

The incubus is a spirit appearing as a male figure, a demon lover who seduces sleeping women and has intercourse with them. (*See also* **Succubus**—a demon

lover appearing to men as a female.) The name comes from the Latin *in*, meaning "on top of" and *cubo* meaning "I lie." The belief in incubi was strong in medieval Europe, and it was thought that any misshapen child was the result of such a union. Variations on this belief are found around the world, in all cultures. The child of a union between an incubus and a mortal woman is known as a *cambion*. It was said that Merlin—magician to the legendary King Arthur—was a cambion.

An incubus supposedly has an ice-cold penis. All energy is drained from the victim, leaving the woman extremely debilitated. It is said that repeated intercourse with an incubus can bring about death.

It was thought by some that incubi and succubi (male and female) were all the same demon or spirit, taking on a different form depending upon whether or not it was seducing a human male or female. A succubus would then obtain semen from a male victim and deposit it in a female victim.

Kachina

The name *Kachina* (*Katsina*; *Qatsina*), in Native American Hopi and Zuni, means "life bringer" and can be anything from a concept to a natural phenomenon. They represent various beings, from animals to clouds. They are supernatural beings who manifest as messengers from the Spirit World and may bring food and gifts. The Hopi pray to them for good harvests and for prosperous lives. The arrival and departure of these spirits are the reason for elaborate ceremonies among the Pueblo people.

Kachina dolls are traditionally made by the Hopi and Zuni Native American people of Arizona. There are well over four hundred different Kachinas, many of them tied in to the passing year. The dolls are traditionally carved from cottonwood root and are kept in the homes of religious Hopi and Zuni families.

The Zuni believe that the Kachinas live in the "Lake of the Dead," which is reached through Listening Spring Lake (at the junction of the Little Colorado River and the Zuni River). In Hopi myths, the Kachina live on the San Francisco Peaks, near Flagstaff, Arizona.

Kan Hotidan

The name means "tree dweller" in Native American lore. This spirit lives in tree stumps from where it directs magic at passersby. This magic can ensure success in hunting but can also be malevolent in nature. Trees are favorite homes for a variety of nature spirits besides the Kan Hotidan.

Kelpie

A Scottish water spirit that appears as a gray horse. It is an omen of death and frequently the cause of death, forcing the observer into the water of a lake or stream, drowning them and then eating them.

A Kelpie lives on the west coast of the Isle of Skye, at Loch Coruisk. There is another in Aberdeen, in the northeast, at Corgaff.

Knocker

Knockers, or Knackers, live in the tin mines of Devon and Cornwall, England. They frequently guide the miners by knocking on the walls of the mine, taking them to rich seams. The miners must then reward them with gifts of food, especially Cornish pasties. They do not like to hear whistling and will cause a fall of rock on the person doing the whistling. Knockers can be seen in the dim light of the tunnels and are described as being thin, small and ugly, with slit mouths and hook noses.

Kobold

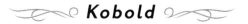

Kobold, or *Kobalt*, is a spirit found in Germany, Austria, Denmark, Sweden, and Switzerland. It can be a mine spirit, much like the Knockers of England, but may also be a house spirit. It is said that a Kobold may be caught in the woods at midsummer, if a bird is found on an anthill. The bird is actually a Kobold in disguise. By talking to the bird, it's possible to relax him and then you can trap him in a bag and take him home. If you treat him well, he will do work around the house and generously reward you.

Lares

Lares (singular: *Lar*) were the protective spirits of ancient Rome (*Lars familiaris*). They were household spirits and were found in every home. Some modern-day Italians claim to see them on occasion. They are friendly to those who live in the house but are antagonistic to strangers.

Larvae

This is a house spirit that is sometimes heard in the house of a smith or other artisan. It is never seen, but it can be heard working, using the smith's tools to create objects that are later discovered.

Liekko

The *Liekko* (meaning "flaming one") is found in Finnish folklore. It is much like the British jack-o'-lantern, being a spectral light that is seen at night and that can lure travelers into unsafe areas. The Liekko is believed to be the spirit of a child who has been buried in the forest. It is an omen of death or disaster to see a Liekko.

Manes

In both ancient and modern Rome, the *Manes* were and are spirits of the dead. They are benevolent spirits, watching over the living. *Manism* refers to these spirits. Manism is a belief that there is an existence after the transition known as "death." The spirits of the deceased will continue to protect and advise the living.

Pooka; *Púca*

A legendary spirit of Irish folklore that can change its shape, favoring that of a horse, dog, rabbit, or goat. Its fur is always dark and its eyes glowing yellow. If, as a horse, a person is enticed onto its back, they will be in for a wild ride though without the Pooka doing the rider any actual harm. The Pooka has the power of human speech, and there are records of it having given good advice and even of it having led people away from dangerous situations. The Pooka has been known to save cattle from drowning. If treated with respect, the Pooka will reward those it encounters. It lives in the woods on the sides of mountains.

Pretu; *Preta*

The Hindus believe that the *Pretu* is the form taken by the soul after death. It is a departed spirit; a ghost . . . the size of a man's thumb! The spirit remains in this state for one year, wandering around its old home. This is also the term used for the ghost of a crippled person or a child who dies prematurely.

Preta are ghosts that live at crossroads and, sometimes, gather outside houses. These ghosts are living out a karma because of envy or the refusal of alms when alive. They are hungry and thirsty, and the performance of Shraddhu will eventually relieve them. In a different body, the soul will enter the true afterlife.

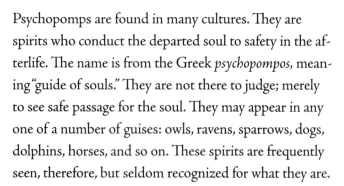

Psychopomp

Psychopomps are found in many cultures. They are spirits who conduct the departed soul to safety in the afterlife. The name is from the Greek *psychopompos*, meaning "guide of souls." They are not there to judge; merely to see safe passage for the soul. They may appear in any one of a number of guises: owls, ravens, sparrows, dogs, dolphins, horses, and so on. These spirits are frequently seen, therefore, but seldom recognized for what they are.

Rusalka

In Russia, a *Rusalka* is the ghost of a young woman who has drowned, either accidentally or been drowned on purpose. The spirit appears as a beautiful and gentle water nymph with long green hair. In secret, the Rusalki help the fisherfolk, who are very poor throughout the area of the Alluvial Islands of southern Russia. It is said that the best time to see a Rusalka—they are very shy—is at the time of Pentecost or Whitsuntide. They swim and float in the water and may balance themselves on tree branches. They bathe in rivers and lakes and dry out their hair on the green banks.

Shíwanna

The *Shíwanna* are the "Cloud People" of Pueblo mythology. They are also known as *Katsína* and

Kópishtaia. They live near a spring or lake, in the mountains, or they may be found near a town close to the sea. Clouds represent the spirits of the dead. When clouds form over the mountains, it is seen as the Shíwanna rising from the water. Shíwanna dances take place from August to November and stop at the first severe frost.

Silkies

Silkies are female spirits found along the borders of England and Scotland. They are small and dainty and dress in gray or white silk. Denton Hall, in Northumberland, England, is said to have been haunted by Silkies. They were happy to work for the Hoyle family, who lived in the Hall, doing housework and placing flowers on the staircase. But after World War II a new family moved in and paid no respect to the Silkies. Consequently the Silkies took on poltergeist behavior to such an extent that the new tenants had to move out!

Spunkie

Scottish Spunkies are very short but have very long arms. They can be extremely unpleasant. They are mostly found on farms in Scotland, though there is a variety of Spunkie found in the southwest of England, in Devon and Cornwall. They will sometimes appear at night, carrying lights so that they are mistaken for Will-o'-the-Wisps.

They then lead the unwary into bogs and ditches. The best time to see them is at Midsummer's Eve.

Succubus

The female equivalent of the incubus (*see* **Incubus**). The *succubus* (Latin: "I lie beneath") is a female-appearing spirit who enters the bed of a man and seduces him. The belief in incubi and succubi was strong in medieval Europe, and it was thought that any misshapen child was the result of such a union; the child being known as a *cambion*. Some thought that incubi and succubi were all the same demon or spirit, taking on a different form depending on which gender it was seducing. A succubus would then obtain semen from a male victim and deposit it in a female victim.

Tadebtsois

The Samoyeds of Siberia believe in the *Tadebtsois*. These were invisible spirits that forever encircled the world in the atmosphere and were a menace to the living. The Siberian shaman who appeased these spirits was known as the *tadibe;* he dressed in reindeer leather trimmed with red cloth. He also wore a mask of red cloth and a breastplate of polished metal. He used a large, flat drum and a rattle to influence the Tadebtsois. In the course of his rituals, the *tadibe* entered a trance and received oracular messages from the Tadebtsois.

Tomga

Familiar spirit of the Eskimos or Inuit. It is contacted by a shaman who proceeds in many ways like a Spiritualist deep-trance medium, with totally different voices coming to answer questions.

Whirlwinds

Whirlwinds are associated with spirits of the dead in Native American lore. Some tribes, such as the Shoshoni of Colorado and Wyoming and the Gros Ventre of Montana, believe that they are apparitions of the deceased and that they may be dangerous.

Wiitiko

In Algonquian folklore, the *Wiitiko* is a spirit that may inhabit the body of an Ojibwa hunter and cause him to adopt cannibalistic traits. The spirit only possesses a hunter who has been repeatedly unsuccessful in the hunt and is consequently ravenously hungry.

Wild Hunt

In much of Europe, thunderstorms were once explained as being a "Wild Hunt" indulged in by the dead. Huge groups of huntsmen and women, horses and hounds, swept across the skies in mad pursuit of an unseen prey.

It was firmly believed that the hunters were the spirits of the dead. The leader would be identified variously in different locales: Woden, Odin, Arawn, Dietrich of Berne, Alemannic, Heren, Valdemar Atterdag, and so on. In some locations the hunt was more specifically referred to as Woden's Hunt, Holda's Hunt, Cain's Hunt, Herod's Hunt, Herlathing, Mesnée d'Hellequin, Cŵn Annwn, Gabriel's Hounds, and so on. To actually see the Wild Hunt was to know that some disaster of national proportions was imminent: war, pestilence, plague, death. In a violent storm, many would cover their heads so that they would not see the hunt.

The Peterborough Abbey Account of February 1127 speaks of hideous black hunters on black horses, accompanied by goats and rams as well as black hounds. The account says that the procession lasted, off and on, throughout Lent and Easter. In contrast, Robert Graves (*The White Goddess*, 1948) speaks of "the Hounds of Hell with white bodies and red eyes."

In sixteenth-century England, when the Church of England split from the Roman Catholic Church, the Wild Hunt was thought to include the spirits of the unbaptized: adults and especially children.

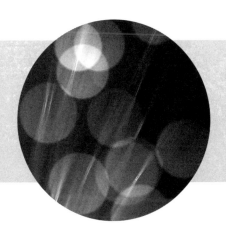

Spectral Lights

Orbs, ghost lights, spheres, fireballs—all these and more are inhuman yet may haunt sites in the same way that ghosts of the deceased do. For centuries they have been reported, frequently associated with spirits of the dead, with nature spirits, and with otherworldly beings. In Ireland, for example, the lights are faeries; in Asia they're gods; and in America they're the ghosts of Native Americans. Famously, there are the Min Min lights of Australia, the Bung Fai Phaya Nak in Thailand, the Hessdalen in Norway, and the Hornet Spooklight and Marfa lights in North America. There are also innumerable sites in Great Britain.

Bung Fai Phaya Nak

These are the "Naga" fireballs of Thailand. They are seen every October emerging from the Mekong River;

anywhere from 200 to 800 of them have been recorded along the 100-kilometer stretch of water. Because of this, as many as 400,000 people visit the river to catch sight of them. They appear in the early evening. Fewer appear in rainy weather than in dry weather. Local legend says that the fireballs are from the *nak,* a serpent from Buddhist legend. Thailand officials claim that they are produced by natural methane gas released from the water, but some experts say that bubbles of methane could not be propagated by the river.

Ghost Lights; Spirit lights

There are many locations in the United States, and around the world, where mysterious lights are seen. They are termed ghost lights, spirit lights, spook lights, and similar. Many have local names. In North Carolina are seen the Maco Station light and the Brown Mountain light; in Misssouri the Hornet Spooklight; Texas has the Marfa lights (*see page 156*) and Anson light, Colorado the Silver Cliff lights, Washington the Yakima lights, North Carolina the Brown Mountain lights, Maryland the Hebron light, Arkansas the Dover light, Hawaii the Waimea lights, and there is the St. Louis light in Saskatchewan, Canada. One of the most famous American lights is found at what is known as the Spooksville Triangle, in the tristate area of Missouri, Oklahoma, and Arkansas.

Hessdalen

The Hessdalen Valley is in central Norway, southwest of Trondheim. It is seven and a half miles long with 200 inhabitants, and is best known for the ghost lights seen there. They were the first such sightings to be subjected to scientific scrutiny when various groups focused a battery of high-tech instruments on the mysterious lights. Nothing substantial was established.

The lights were first noticed in 1981, suddenly appearing low in the sky over the valley. They are mostly stationary but have been seen to move slowly and, occasionally, at high speed. Photographs show that they vary in color and shape, the three main shapes being like an upside-down Christmas tree, a round orb, and a bullet-shape with the pointed end down. Colors are yellow-white with occasional blue flashes and glimpses of red.

Ignis Fatuus

The name *ignis fatuus* means "the foolish fire" and is applied to those spook lights that attract travelers and cause them to follow, usually to their detriment. They appear as blue or yellow flames or globes and seem to mysteriously float above the surface of the ground, bobbing about like balloons on a string. They are not peculiar to any one area but are found around the world. Local legends often tie in the lights to stories of suicides, murders, and mysterious deaths, also with unbaptized infants and with people who have drowned in the local bogs. Frequently the claims are that the light represents a spirit in torment doomed to roam the countryside forever. In Native American lore (Penobscot), the light is an omen of death known as "fire demon."

Jack-o'-Lantern

In Britain, the Jack-o'-lantern is a form of *ignis fatuus* (*see 155*) frequently seen floating over marshy places. In German folklore, it is known as *Dickenpoten* and is thought to be the soul of someone condemned to wander over the land to atone for various misdeeds. Although Jack-o'-lanterns are best known for leading people astray, there have been instances when they have appeared and led people to safety. Although often explained away as "swamp gas" or the like, these balls of light seem to have intelligence and are able to take a course that does not follow any possible line of gas emission.

Marfa Lights

First reported in 1883, the Marfa lights are seen to the southwest of the Chinati Mountains, Texas, near U.S. Routes 90 and 67 on Mitchell Flat. They appear like brightly illuminated spheres the size of baseballs and up to basketballs. They float above the ground and sometimes go high into the air. They vary in color: red, orange, yellow, green, and blue, and they may shoot off rapidly in any direction without warning. They may be individual lights, or they may appear in pairs or groups. The Marfa lights are seen only at night, dusk to dawn (never in the daytime), in all seasons regardless of the weather. They appear ten to twenty times a year. They may remain visible for only a few seconds or for a number of hours. The lights have been described as like a fireworks display but without the noise and smoke.

There have been similar lights seen in the area stretching from El Paso southeastward along the Rio Grande Valley, past Big Bend National Park, and farther southeastward into Mexico.

Min Min Lights

The Min Min lights are found in Boulia, southwest Queensland, Australia. They are named after the hotel from which they were first sighted. *Min* is an Aboriginal word. Aboriginal folklore predating Western settlement of the region contains stories about the lights, which sometimes seem to follow people, or approach them and then disappear. Professor Jack Pettigrew, of the University of Queensland, in 2003 produced a study claiming that the Min Min lights were caused by refracted lights from up to 300 kilometers away, made visible by temperature inversions. He reproduced the lights with his car headlights. However, the lights have been seen since before there were cars and their headlights in the area. Travelers say that their horses are unaffected by the lights.

Orbs; Spheres

Orbs seem to have become very prominent with the growth of digital cameras. However, they have also been picked up on 35mm film cameras. Interestingly, the orbs are never in the same place in two consecutive pictures, removing the explanation of dirt mites, or similar, to explain the pictures. In fact, many times there may be perfectly clear photographs, in addition to those containing orbs, which were taken at the same time. Dave Juliano, on his Web site (*www.theshadowlands.net*), says:

> I took a 35mm camera that I had used regularly for 6 years in all types of lighting and weather and had never gotten an orb or other unexplainable photo before, and went out with a few seasoned field investigators on a cemetery investigation. One of the investigators was psychic and she pointed out a few areas we should take photos, so I did. I also heard ghost footsteps walk up behind me twice and I turned around quickly and took photos of the empty air. When I got my photos developed, I had these orbs and fog in those photos that I was told to take, as well as the footstep ones. All my other photos were normal.

The jury is certainly still out on the cause of orbs. It seems there may well be logical explanations for many of them. But it seems equally certain that others cannot be easily explained. There is the strong possibility that a large number of orbs do indeed indicate metaphysical energy if not definite spirit presence. Ghost faces, along with symbols and other signs, have been found on the enlarged images of orbs. Photographs taken at known haunted sites and historical sites seem to be especially prone to produce orbs and spheres.

With the initial acceptance of orbs as a psychic or spiritual phenomenon, there is now deeper examination being undertaken, with scrutiny of aspects such as the meaning of particular colors. Colors have always had "traditional" meanings—as in candle-burning magic and color-healing magic—though there is no one definitive listing of such meanings. Native Americans have certain interpretations for the different colors; Chinese and other Asians have different interpretations; the West has a number of separate schools of thought on it. This all makes the color of orbs an interesting topic—especially where the photographic site and its history may have bearing on what is obtained.

Vortex Ghosts; Funnel Ghosts

Most often seen in old buildings and ruins, these ghosts are only occasionally found in the outdoors.

They take the appearance of a swirling vortex or funnel, much like a miniature tornado. Many times the appearance of a funnel ghost is followed by the manifestation of orbs, and it has been suggested that the vortex is a vehicle to transport spirits in the form of orbs.

Will-o'-the-Wisp

Known by a wide variety of names, the Will-o'-the-Wisp is another of those *ignis fatuus* lights that seem to have no scientific explanation. The Will-o'-the-Wisp has been recorded as flickering over marshy ground at least since the Middle Ages. People have attempted to explain it away by saying that it is marsh gas: methane or phosphorus hydride or similar. Yet the lights themselves do not follow any typical pattern for these gases, emitting no heat and moving freely in any direction. They have been said to signify unmarked graves, to be the sign of mischievous nature spirits, to be "corpse candles" (tied in to suicides and murders), to mark the site of buried treasure, and to be the work of fairies.

The word *wisp* comes from the word for a bundle of straw, sticks, or paper—a "whisper" of a larger amount—used as a torch to light the way. In Finland it was thought that Midsummer was the best time to look for Will-o'-the-Wisps that marked buried treasure. The Swedes, Danes, Estonians, and Latvians believed that this treasure could only be taken when the light was there. The light is known as *Gandaspati* in

Indonesia and Central Java and is thought to be a flame able to take the form of a dragon. It will kill anyone who touches it.

In Guernsey it's known as the *faeu boulanger*, the "rolling fire," and is thought to be a lost soul. Meeting such a phenomenon, the only way to be safe is to turn your coat or your hat inside out. Alternatively, you can place a knife in the ground with the blade pointing up. This will attract the *faeu*, who will attack the blade rather than the person.

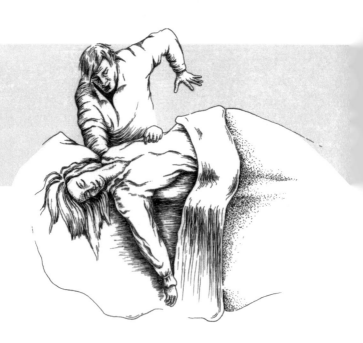

Vampires

*Any mention of vampires leads many people to imme-
diately think of Count Dracula, the antagonist in Bram
Stoker's 1897 gothic horror novel. But there have been
stories of bloodsucking vampires in many cultures. Some
of these have been human—or the spirits of humans—
while others have been entirely nonhuman. Bloodsucking
vampire bats are a reality, in South America, but their
victims are mainly cattle. The vampire as one who has
come back from the dead is a superstition found especially in Slavic culture, and is the pervading superstition
now found almost universally.*

Hag; Old Hag

The "Old Hag of the Dribble" (*gwrach-y-rhibyn*), who is one of the Welsh banshees, wails and flaps her raven wings against the window of those who are doomed to die. The Old Hags (of various locations and cultures) can act like poltergeists, causing things to fly through the air, pictures to fall from walls, and crockery to break. They may also have vampire characteristics, attacking sleeping persons and leaving them drained of all energy. The term *hag* might be short for *hægtesse,* an Old English term for a witch. In British folklore, the Old Hag sits on the chest of a sleeping person, sending them nightmares and making it difficult to breathe or even move. This was referred to as being "hagridden." There have been reports of hags and being hagridden since earliest times.

In Scottish and Irish mythology, the hag is the *Cailleach,* a goddess concerned with weather, harvest, and creation. She works with the goddess Bride, being dominant in the winter months while Bride is to the fore in the summer.

La Llorona

In Mexican folklore, *La Llorona* is "The Weeper" or "The Weeping Woman." She is the ghost of a mother who is searching for her murdered child (*see* **Apparitions**).

She may be seen as a hitchhiker at the side of the road (or even in the very middle of the road) and be

picked up, or she may suddenly appear inside the moving car. She is sometimes described as beautiful and seductive, and she wears either a white dress or a black one. She has long black hair and very long fingernails. She usually appears to a man who is driving alone. He will often remember nothing until he finds himself sitting alone in his vehicle at the side of the road, feeling completely exhausted as though his life has been drained from him.

Tii

The *Tii* is a Polynesian vampire. A once-living person, it is a soulless spirit that feeds on the blood of the living.

Warning Ghosts

As their name implies, Warning Ghosts are those that appear, or make themselves known in some way, as a warning to the observer of impending danger or even death. In this way they are a variety of Omen Ghosts but are more specific. For example, the ghost of someone's grandfather warning of coming death or injury to the grandson or granddaughter. There is, then, a specific connection between the ghost and the observer.

Practical Ghost Hunting

Knowing of the many different types of ghosts, and knowing also of some of the most haunted sites, the next logical step would seem to be to go looking for ghosts. And why not? There is a big interest in ghost hunting these days, with a number of television series devoted to it and large numbers of Internet Web sites dealing with the issue. Many areas have local ghost-hunting or paranormal-investigating clubs and societies.

Ghost hunting need not be expensive. You can certainly spend a lot on such things as thermal imaging devices, computer hardware and software, electro-magnetic field (EMF) detectors, laser grids, video and recording equipment, but you don't *have* to.

The first item you should have is a notebook and pencil, for record keeping is the most important part of ghost hunting. Always log the date of the investigation, the location or address, the person or people involved, and previously observed phenomena. Make a diagram of the site with notes as to what has been seen and/or heard in the past, by whom, and when. Get the names of anyone involved, such as the home owner if a home. (Do not publish these names without permission from the people; you can obtain this with a release form.) It's a good idea to have two or three colored pens or pencils available, so that a variety of movements or similar notes can be indicated on the site map without getting too confusing.

Measuring tape is essential, for accuracy with regard to movements, distance of sighting, movements of objects, and so on. A flashlight can be most useful (with extra batteries). A camera should be used—even a cheap one, though a more sophisticated one is best. On the subject of photography, it can be very helpful to have more than one camera: a regular film camera, such as a 35mm, loaded with a fast (at least 400ASA) film; a similar one loaded with infrared film if at all possible; and a modern digital camera. Additionally, a video camera can be a plus. If all else fails, don't hesitate to take pictures with a camera cell phone. Any record is better than none.

One instrument that is very useful, and not too expensive, is an electromagnetic field (EMF) meter. This will indicate an interruption or disruption in the magnetic field at a location. There are also some portable motion detectors that are not too expensive. A great many paranormal phenomena are accompanied by a noticeable drop in temperature. To have a thermometer along with you can be useful, and you should record in your notebook any temperature changes. Along the same lines, an infrared motion detector can be very worthwhile.

Sound recording devices are good to have, especially if the ghost is audible rather than, or in addition to being, visible. If you use a tape recorder, use one with two speeds; recording at the higher speed so that you can later play back at the lower speed. But most EVP (electronic voice phenomena) researchers these days use digital recorders.

If there is more than one investigator at a site, then the use of two-way radios can be very useful. Do not use cell phones for this, since they can give off an electromagnetic pulse that will interfere with the meters. Keep any such communication to a minimum.

Start your investigation with an open mind. A certain amount of skepticism is in order; you should not be gullible, believing everything that witnesses tell you. This is not to say that witnesses lie—though, of course, some do (see *Amityville Horror*)—but some want desperately to believe in ghosts, or to believe that their house is haunted, to the point that they may *unconsciously* stretch the truth! Don't go looking for ghosts. . . . Go to examine the evidence that will help you determine whether or not there *is* a ghost. If there is more than one witness, interview them separately. If there is only one witness, have someone else in addition to yourself interview that person. Record all testimony.

EMFs

Electromagnetic field meters are the most commonly used instruments in ghost hunting these days. There are various ones available, from inexpensive (about $30) to very expensive ($200–$300). There is even one marketed as a "ghost meter"! The EMF measures VLF (very low frequency) and ELF (extremely low frequency) magnetic radiation on both low and high settings, in mG (milligauss—a gauss is a unit of magnetic field strength measurement). There are also alternating current (AC) and direct current (DC) meters and some that will also register temperature. Ghost hunter and official historian at Lily Dale, New York (the oldest and largest Spiritualist community in the world), Ron Nagy says that there is a discussion going on as to whether DC can pick up on a paranormal field. Some say AC is best because it will register paranormal activity more accurately, but the jury is out on that point.

The meter should be carried in one hand, extended out in front of you as you move slowly around the haunted site. With many meters, be careful not to cover the end with your fingers, since that will interfere with the readings, and do not hold it too close to your body. You can "scan" the area by moving the meter in an arc from side to side as you move forward. If the meter indicates a sudden burst of energy, there is always the possibility that you are picking up from some electrical appliance or outlet. Double-check for natural explanations before assuming supernatural ones.

If you get a positive reading on the meter, that is otherwise unexplainable, then (1) take photographs in the direction it is pointing, (2) check with your thermometer for a temperature drop, and (3) make sure your audio recorder is running. (It's best to have that recording all the time.)

The EMF is a delicate instrument and should be treated with respect. Handle it gently, and don't make any sharp and sudden movements with it.

Cameras

As mentioned, it is a good plan to have a number of cameras, or at the very least both a film camera and a digital one. As with all matters photographic, the more expensive the equipment, the better the results. But this doesn't mean that you can't get some sort of results with very inexpensive cameras. Some really excellent ghost photographs have been caught on "throwaway" cameras, for example. However, with a 35mm single-lens reflex, you can vary the settings, both of speed and aperture. A fast film (such as 400ASA) is recommended, especially for poorly lit areas.

One aspect that seems seldom addressed is that of filters. A polarizing filter is strongly recommended; this will prevent reflections, so often interpreted as "ghost" presences. Special filters are needed for infrared film (which requires special handling in every way—even loading the camera, which must be done in absolute darkness).

If possible, set up a camera on a stable bed (for example, a tripod) with a wide-angle lens that will include a good range of the field you're studying. A video camera set up this way is good, since you can get it going and leave it running. One advantage of a video camera is that most models these days have an infrared setting (sometimes called "Nightshot"), allowing shooting in the dark.

Do make sure that your camera lens is clean and that your flash, if you are using one, is not going to reflect off something back into the camera lens. Try to get clear, sharp, *in focus* shots and make sure that nothing is dangling in front of the lens (such as a camera strap, finger, or length of hair!).

EVP Recorders

Electronic voice phenomena can be recorded on tape or digital recorders, but it has been found that the digital recorders are far superior. Of these, the IC (Integrated Circuit) recorders are best. A good inexpensive IC recorder is the Panasonic RR-US380, which is small but extremely effective. An early model that was very much respected was the Panasonic RR-DR60.

If you are using tape, make sure you have a very good microphone. If it's a cassette tape recorder or any other with a built-in microphone, use a plug-in instead of the built-in so that you don't pick up the hum of the machine itself. With IC recorders, there is no mechanical noise, so you don't need the external microphone. When playing back, it's a good idea to use earphones, since many times the EVP is hard to hear.

The AA-EVP Web site on the Internet (*www.aaevp.com*) is the very best source for information on EVP and ITC (instrumental transcommunication—to include such examples as video pictures, computer messages, radio, spirit telephone, and faxes, and so on). To quote from the AA-EVP site:

> You can substitute a computer for the tape recorder if you wish. Your computer should have an audio input jack, speakers, headphone jack and sound player application of some form. Windows comes with a sound recorder application that will work. A sound editor like *Audition* or *Audacity* is most popular because these applications allow for easy amplification, filtering, and reversing of the sound files.

You can either make the recording on a tape recorder and then play the tape into the computer for review, editing and storage, or attach a microphone directly to the computer and use the sound editor as a tape recorder. When transferring into a computer, make sure the computer is set for "Line In" recording in "Sound and Multimedia" in the Control Panel of your Personal Computer. If you must take sound from the "Earphone" jack of your recorder, consider purchasing an "attenuating cord" to match the difference in resistance between the two jacks.

Infrared Thermometer

These range in price from $15 to $1,500 . . . but an inexpensive one will do fine. They are sometimes termed "noncontact thermometers," since they can record temperature changes without actually being in contact with the object (such as a ghost!). Consequently the infrared thermometer is useful for measuring temperature under circumstances where other probe-type sensors cannot be used or do not produce accurate data. Some typical circumstances are when the object to be measured is moving; when the object is surrounded by an electromagnetic field; when the object is contained in a vacuum or other controlled atmosphere; or in applications when a fast response is required.

Passive Infrared
Motion Detector

Passive infrared motion detectors (PIRs) are inexpensive enough that two or three can be bought and used. They can be useful to set up at a haunting where you want to be sure that there is no outside interference and no fraud. You should use detectors that are set off not only by motion but also by temperature change. Apparent motion is detected when an infrared source with one temperature, such as a human, passes in front of an infrared source with another temperature, such as a wall. All objects emit what is known as "black body radiation"—energy that is invisible to the human eye. The term *passive* in this instance means the PIR does not emit energy of any type but merely accepts incoming infrared radiation.

Computer

The use of a laptop computer, although by no means essential, can be an intriguing accessory. In the mid-1980s, in England, in the days before there were laptops and before there were desktops in every home, Ken Webster borrowed a computer from the school where he taught and worked on it at home. He was amazed to suddenly get messages from a departed spirit—a spirit from the sixteenth century! (This was also in the days before e-mails and computer hacking and the like.) The spirit was a Thomas Harding who wrote on the computer to complain about Webster living in his (Harding's) home! The house did indeed date back to the sixteenth century. Research at Oxford Library confirmed the language, dialect, spelling, style, and so on of the messages as being of that period.

In the early days of Spiritualism, at a séance it was common practice to set out two school slates. At the start of the sitting they would be tied together, with a small piece of chalk between them, and then they'd be opened up again at the end. Invariably it was found that the spirits had written a message on one or both of the slates. With a laptop computer set up at a haunt site, it is possible to have a modern version of the Spiritualist slates, to receive messages from the ghosts there. Request them to write to you in, say, a simple text program like Wordpad. Or you can open a special folder in such a program as Microsoft Word and dedicate it to ghostly correspondence. Close the laptop at the start of your ghost hunting and then open it again at the very end to see if there is any message from the spirits in your program.

Compass

Not an essential piece of equipment, but an interesting tool is a compass. Many times paranormal activity that does not reflect on, say, an EMF may still cause the needle of an ordinary compass to suddenly spin. The needle may also swing in the direction of a ghost and indicate its movements.

Record Keeping

Record keeping is one of the most important parts of ghost hunting. Especially note dates and times of the day and/or night. Give exact locations: addresses and/ or map references if needed. Interview witnesses and get their stories, then *get them to sign them as accurate.* List the ghost hunters involved. Reference your photographs and sound recordings. Note what film was used and what exposures, also what recording tape.

Research

You can never do too much research. Research as much as possible before the investigation and follow up afterward, checking what is discovered. Many psychics don't want to know anything about it ahead of time, so that they are not influenced, but serious ghost hunters are not testing themselves; they are investigating a haunting. Knowledge of the history of the site can be very useful.

Further Reading

Asala, Joanne (ed.). *Scandinavian Ghost Stories*. New York: William Morrow, 1974.

Auerbach, Lloyd. *ESP, Hauntings and Poltergeists*. New York: Warner Books, 1986.

Bander, Peter. *Voices from the Tapes: Recording from the Other World*. New York: Drake, 1973.

Bardens, Dennis. *Ghosts and Hauntings*. London: Taplinger, 1968.

Blackman, W. Haden. *The Field Guide to North American Ghosts*. New York: Three Rivers Press, 1998.

Bletzer, June G. *The Encyclopedic Psychic Dictionary*. Lithia Springs: New Leaf, 1986.

Bord, Janet and Colin. *The World of the Unexplained*. London: Blandford, 1998.

Briggs, Katharine. *An Encyclopedia of Fairies: Hobgoblins, Brownies, Bogies, and Other Supernatural Creatures*. New York: Pantheon, 1976.

Buckland, Raymond. *Buckland Book of Spirit Communications*. St. Paul: Llewllyn, 2004.

———. *The Spirit Book*. Detroit: Visible Ink Press, 2006.

———. *The Truth about Spirit Communication*. St. Paul: Llewellyn, 1995.

Buckland, Raymond, and Hereward Carrington. *Amazing Secrets of the Psychic World*. Parker Publishing, New York 1975.

Butler, Tom and Lisa. *There Is No Death and There Are No Dead*. Reno: AA-EVP, 2003.

Caidin, Martin. *Ghosts of the Air*. St. Paul: Galde Press, 1995.

Citro, Joseph A. *The Vermont Ghost Guide*. Lebanon: University Press of New England, 2000.

Clyne, Patricia Edwards. *Ghostly Animals of America*. New York: Dodd, Mead, 1977.

Cohen, Daniel. *The Encyclopedia of Ghosts*. New York: Dodd, Mead, 1984.

Coulombe, Charles A. *Haunted Castles of the World*. Guilford: Lyons Press, 2004.

Danelek, J. Allan. *The Case For Ghosts*. Woodbury: Llewellyn, 2006.

Denning, Hazel M. *True Hauntings*. St. Paul: Llewellyn, 1996.

Flammarion, Camille. *Haunted Houses*. London: T. Fisher Unwin, 1924.

Floyd, Randall. *Ghost Lights and Other Encounters*. Little Rock: August House, 1993.

Gauld, Alan, and A. D. Cornell. *Poltergeists*. London: Routledge & Kegan Paul, 1979.

Gettings, Fred. *Ghosts in Photographs*. New York: Harmony Books, 1978.

Goodwin, Melba. *Ghost Worlds*. Woodbury: Llewellyn, 2007.

Grant, Douglas. *The Cock Lane Ghost*. New York: St. Martin's Press, 1965.

Green, Celia, and Charles McCreery. *Apparitions*. London: Hamish Hamilton, 1975.

Guiley, Rosemary Ellen. *The Encyclopedia of Ghosts and Spirits*. New York: Facts on File, 1992.

Haining, Peter. *A Dictionary of Ghost Lore*. New York: Prentice-Hall, 1984.

Hole, Christina. *Haunted England*. London: Scribners, 1941.

Holzer, Hans. *Ghosts, Hauntings and Possessions*. St. Paul: Llewellyn, 1990.

———. *The Great British Ghost Hunt*. Boston: G. K. Hall, 1975.

———. *The Lively Ghosts of Ireland*. New York: Ace Books, 1967.

———. *Westghosts*. Chicago: Swallow Press, 1980.

———. *Yankee Ghosts*. New York: Ace Books, 1966.

Iremonger, Lucille. *The Ghosts of Versailles*. London: Faber & Faber, 1957.

Kachuba, John. *Ghost Hunters*. Franklin Lakes: New Page Books, 2007.

Knight, David C. *Poltergeists: Hauntings and the Haunted*. New York: J. B. Lippincott, 1972.

Leach, Maria (ed.). *Funk & Wagnalls Standard Dictionary of Folklore, Mythology, and Legend*. San Francisco: Harper & Row, 1972.

MacKenzie, Andrew. *Hauntings and Apparitions*. London: Heinemann, 1982.

Maple, Eric. *The Realm of Ghosts*. London: A. S. Barnes, 1964.

Mead, Robin. *Haunted Hotels*. Nashville: Rutledge Hill Press, 1995.

Morrow, Ed. *The Halloween Handbook*. New York: Citadel Press, 2001.

Nesbitt, Mark. *Ghosts of Gettysburg*. Gettysburg: Thomas Publications, 1991.

———. *More Ghosts of Gettysburg*. Gettysburg: Thomas Publications, 1992.

Price, Harry. *The Most Haunted House in England*. London: Longmans, Green, 1940.

Reader's Digest. *Into the Unknown*. Pleasantville: Reader's Digest, 1981.

Roll, William George. *The Poltergeist*. New York: Doubleday, 1972.

Shephard, Leslie A. (ed.). *Encyclopedia of Occultism and Parapsychology*. New York: Avon, 1978.

Sitwell, Sacheverell. *Poltergeists*. New York: University Books, 1959.

Smith, Suzie. *Haunted Houses for the Millions*. Los Angeles: Sherbourne Press, 1967.

Steiger, Brad. *Monsters Among Us*. New York: Berkley Books, 1989.

———. *Real Ghosts, Restless Spirits, and Haunted Places*. Detroit: Visible Ink Press, 2003.

Taylor, Troy. *Ghost Hunter's Guidebook*. Decatur: Whitechapel, 2007.

Tyrell, G. N. M. *Apparitions*. London: Society for Psychical Research, 1953.

Underwood, Peter. *The Ghost Hunters*. London: Robert Hale, 1985.

———. *Haunted London*. London: George C. Harrup, 1973.

Walker, Danton. *I Believe In Ghosts*. New York: Taplinger, 1969.

Warren, Ed and Lorraine. *Ghost Hunters*. New York: St. Martin's Press, 1989.

Warren, Joshua. Pet Ghosts: *Animal Encounters*. Franklin Lakes: New Page Books, 2006.

Willin, Melvyn. *Ghosts Caught on Film*. Cincinnati: David & Charles, 2007.

Winer, Richard. *Ghost Ships*. New York: Berkley Publishing Group, 2000.

Index

About the Author

Raymond Buckland is the author of more than fifty books on occult, witchcraft, and paranormal subjects, including *Buckland's Complete Book of Witchcraft*, *Buckland's Book of Spirit Communications* and *The Spirit Book*. He has been the subject of numerous articles and interviews in such publications as *The New York Times*, *Cosmopolitan*, and *The Los Angeles Times*, and has contributed countless articles to magazines, including *Fate* and *The National Spiritualist Summit*. Over the past forty years he has appeared on television and radio talk shows both in the United States and abroad. He regularly speaks and teaches at Lily Dale Assembly, New York, on the subject of spiritualism, and is popularly known as "The Father of American Wicca." He lives in Ohio. Visit him on the web at: *www.raybuckland.com.*

The Weiser
Field Guide series

For more than fifty years, Weiser Books has published books for seekers and spiritual practitioners from a variety of traditions, from new consciousness to magick to coming earth changes to Western Mystery, Tarot, Astrology, the paranormal, and more. The Weiser Field Guide series developed out of our desire to introduce a new generation of readers and to provide a handbook to esoteric and occult secrets from throughout time and around the world and beyond. We hope these guides entertain and inform.

IN THE SERIES:

The Weiser Field Guide to Ghosts: Apparitions, Sprits, Spectral Lights, and Other Hauntings of History and Legend

The Weiser Field Guide to Vampires: Legends, Practices, and Encounters Old and New

Watch for forthcoming titles.